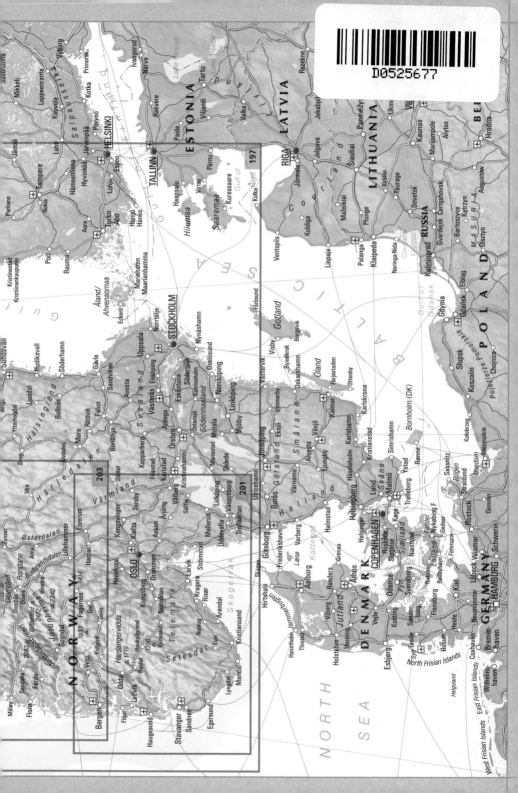

oto Guide

NORWAY

The foot of the massive glacier Melkevollbreen just above the lake of Oldevatnet, on the edge of Jostedalsbreen National Park. Nevertheless, it is merely a branch of the biggest glacier in mainland Europe.

Photo Guide

NORWAY

The sagas, myths, and legends of Europe's extreme north are as mysterious as its serene and mystical landscape, while the legendary – and sometimes endearing, though rather ugly – trolls take pride of place within Norway's folk culture.

Note: To telephone Norway from abroad, dial the international prefix from your country, followed by the code for Norway (47) and then the telephone number required: e.g. international prefix +47 12 34 56 78. Also note that there are no individual area codes for Norway.

PROFILE

THE HIGHLIGHTS

CONTENTS

As lavishly illustrated as a coffee-table book and as informative and practical as a travel guide, this *Photo Guide* is the perfect companion for your visit. Take an atmospheric journey of discovery through the greatest tourist sites in Norway in the "Highlights" section, while in the practical "Explorer" chapter our experts have collated the most interesting sights and attractions, along with a selection of hotels and restaurants within easy reach at each location. There are also descriptions of the most beautiful cities and a selection of driving tours and excursions, followed by a comprehensive atlas section.

NORWAY EXPLORER   ATLAS

This sparsely populated Scandinavian country, whose landscape is shaped by mighty glaciers and deep fjords, is the birthplace of winter sportsmen and poets, and of course also of the Viking warriors of world renown. Nature lovers will find plenty to interest them, while those interested in history and the arts will enjoy exploring the country's many unique stave churches. Although Norway (whose wealth comes from oil production) is relatively secluded geographically, its inhabitants are cosmopolitan and forward-thinking, and proud of their individuality. Although not a member state of the European Union, Norway nevertheless maintains close ties with the Union and its activities and legislation.

The Vega Archipelago (Vegaøyan), made up of a cluster of several dozen islands huddled around the main island Vega (from where the archipelago gets its name), lies just south of the Arctic Circle. The group of islands is a breeding ground for eider ducks, which use their extremely delicate white down feathers to line their nests. These sea-ducks are also prized by humans as their warming down is used to fill pillows, quilts, and snug sleeping bags.

The benefits of the Gulf Stream

The northern part of Norway stretches right into the Arctic. Compared with other similarly situated areas, such as Alaska or the northern expanses of Canada or Siberia, it has a relatively mild climate, allowing settlement even in the polar regions – the most northerly human presence in the world. This is thanks to the Gulf

The tiny fishing port of Hamnøy, on the island of Moskenesøya in the Lofoten archipelago.

Stream, an ocean current bringing relatively warm water northward from the southern tropical zone. This continues as the North Atlantic Drift, which significantly influences the climate of Norway's coastal regions and also keeps most of the ports (even in the north) free of ice all year round. As it continues from the north of Scotland past Norway's Atlantic coast, it is known as the Norwegian Current.

Fascinating diversity

Norway's unique countryside can only be described in superlatives. It features Europe's longest fjord, the highest mountains in Scandinavia, and the largest glacier on mainland Europe, to name but a few of the country's fascinating landmarks. Extensive fjells (plateaus), deep carved valleys, rugged coastlines, broad vistas of inland lakes, endless forests, striking waterfalls, and widely scattered islands are some of the other natural wonders that leave their indelible mark upon this country, sandwiched between the North Sea and Arctic Ocean.
Around a third of Norway's landmass stretches north beyond the Arctic Circle, and even the country's shape itself is worthy of note: at around 1,750 km (1,087 miles) long, its widest point reaches only around 450 km (280 miles) across, down to a mere 6 km (4 miles) at its narrowest.

Mountains and glaciers

The Scandinavian Mountains wind their way across the whole of Norway's territory. To the west, the majority of the landscape slopes off steeply toward the sea. The highest mountain ranges rise up in the south, where the country is broadest. Jotunheimen National Park (containing a mountain formation of the same name) is home to Galdhøppigen, which at 2,469 m (8,100 feet) is the highest peak in northern Europe. The park stretches

westward to meet the Jostedalsbreen, a glacier covering roughly 500 sq. km (193 sq. miles) – within Europe, only Iceland's biggest glaciers surpass it in size. In some parts of the Jostedalsbreen, the ice is up to 500 m (1,640 feet) thick.

The land of 1,000 fjords

Coastal Norway's most striking features are without a doubt the fjords, stretching far inland. Norway has more of these narrow gorges than any other country in the world. They were created during the Ice Age, carved out when the glaciers on the tallest mountains stretched toward the coast, forming river valleys (V-shaped valleys) and so-called trough valleys (U-shaped valleys) along the way. After the Ice Age, melting glaciers caused the sea level to rise, filling these deep channels with water – and so the landscape of the fjords came into being. The Sognefjord, stretching 204 km (127 miles), is the longest such inlet in Europe. With some rock faces towering more than 1,500 m (4,920 feet) above the gorge, there is no better view anywhere in the world.

Bewitched by the light

Norway's particular geographical location means that day and night change length to a remarkable extent over the course of a year. The Arctic Circle marks one specific light boundary: at this latitude, the sun never sets at the height of summer, and at the beginning of winter it

stays correspondingly hidden below the horizon; polar night conquers polar day. Further north, this phenomenon lasts even longer. Summer at the North Cape sees the sun shine for around 80 days without setting, and winter is governed by an equally long period of gloom and darkness.
This "dark" season is the best time of year to see the amazingly spellbinding polar auras that sometimes appear in the sky. Known as the Northern Lights, this spectacle paints a radiant variety of shapes and outlines across the sky, from arcs and bands to cloudlike formations. Although the phenomenon was originally thought to be supernatural, it has now been accounted for by the laws of science – though this has not dented its ability to fascinate.

Vegetation zones

Because Norway stretches a great distance north to south and varies widely in altitude, it boasts many different types of vegetation. In the extreme north, and on the mountain peaks, the landscape is dominated by treeless tundra of dwarf shrubs, moss, and lichen. Areas further south and at lower altitudes are gradually taken over by coniferous woodland, pines, and spruces, with an abundance of berries making such woodland particularly special. The mountain plateaus, ablaze in warm hues during the autumnal months, are home to fjell birch trees and willows. In the south and south-west, deciduous forests of oaks, elms, ashes, and lime trees predominate.

SCENERY AND THE NATURAL WORLD

The animal kingdom – from elk and wolf to polar bear

Elks are mostly found in the forests, whereas reindeer have spread all over Norway, running wild in the south and being used as domesticated animals in the north. Many fjords boast colonies of seals. Some national parks are the natural environment for wild animals such as brown bears, wolves, and lynxes, and the northern part of the mainland is home to various polar animals, including Arctic hares and Arctic foxes. The coastline's many cliffs attract an abundance of seabirds, but the marine world is richer still. Salmon and trout jump in the rivers; the lakes are the dwelling place of pike and carp, with cod and mackerel ruling the seas. The Svalbard archipelago, straddling the North Atlantic and Arctic Oceans, is polar bear territory.

A scattered island world

The nation of Norway is spread over tens of thousands of islands, among which the most famous are Svalbard, the Lofoten archipelago bordering the Vesterålen islands to the north, and the distant Jan Mayen. The heavily glaciated Svalbard island cluster with its chief island Spitsbergen lies 600 km (373 miles) north of the mainland's northernmost point, and the volcanic island Jan Mayen (stretching to 2,277 m/7,470 feet, above sea level) is nearer to Greenland than Norway. The landscape of the Lofoten and Vesterålen islands is much more similar to that of the mainland.

The Nordland province contains the country's narrowest point. Above: The Hamarøy peninsula.

The rugged and ice-covered peaks of Galdhøpiggen (Norway's highest mountain) and Glittertind form a striking crown to the Jotunheimen mountain range.

Fjells are plateaus – bald tundras shaped by an astonishing expanse of fens. Above: The Hidda plateau in Dovrefjell-Sunndalsfjella National Park.

The prehistoric imagery of Alta gives us valuable insight into human activity in northern Europe after the last Ice Age. These rock carvings, discovered in 1973, have been a UNESCO World Heritage Site since 1985. Around 400 carved designs, the oldest of which have been in place more than 60,000 years, feature recurring scenes of daily life, hunts, and animals, and help us to understand the way of life of people at the time.

The Vikings

Generally portrayed as bloodthirsty marauders leaving fear and terror in their wake, there was in fact much more to the Vikings who broke into southern Europe from Scandinavia between the 9th and 11th centuries: they were skilled traders, crafty strategists, founders of cities (including Dublin), and colonial masters (e.g. in Iceland and Greenland). These tough wayfarers are

Inside Lofotr Viking Museum, Borg, Lofoten.

most famous for their mastery of shipbuilding. This success was in no small part due to the robust nature of their slight ships, propelled by up to 50 rowers. Under the leadership of Eirik Torvaldsson – known as Erik the Red because of his striking hair – the Vikings reached Greenland, and Erik's son Leif Eriksson is thought to be the first European to have set foot in North America around 500 years before Christopher Columbus.

From the Bronze Age to the Late Middle Ages

Norway has been shaped by its long, impressive history. Early stone monuments and rock carvings attest to the fact that Norway was already inhabited during the Bronze Age. The first attempt at any unification was made in 872 by Harald Fairhair, who combined several small kingships to create an empire. From the early 9th century, the Vikings began to spread out from Norway toward the North Sea and later the Atlantic, set on conquest, and they soon became masters of the sea – although ironically not for long in their own country, where the Danish began to exert more and more influence. Following the collapse of the empire, King Olav II succeeded in once more unifying the country at the beginning of the 11th century, continuing the Christianization set in motion by his predecessors. The 12th and 13th centuries were plagued by civil unrest. However, the towns and cities soon experienced an upturn of fortune, and the Hanseatic League established commercial settlements along the coast. The territory of Norway began to expand, its system of administration became ever more efficient, and hundreds of stave churches were also constructed.

Swedish and Danish rule

For Norway, the Late Middle Ages were an era of decline. Following the death of Haakon V in 1319, the Nor-wegian crown passed to the Swedish king Magnus Eriks-son, who from that point on ruled the country in union with Sweden. In 1397, his daughter-in-law Queen Mar-garet I of Denmark united the kingdoms of Norway, Swe-den, and Denmark under the banner of the Kalmar Union, ending the period of prosperity that Norway had enjoyed during the previous centuries. It had very little influence in the Union, partly as a result of the disastrous plague epi-demic that devastated the country in the middle of the 14th century, which claimed the lives of more than a third of the population. The rulers of Scandinavia assigned Nor-way little value, and the country's development slowed to a halt. The Kalmar Union came to an end in 1523 when Sweden with-drew, and the royal dynasty of Denmark took over the rule of Norway. This reduced Norway to little more than a Danish province, and as a consequence the country was forced into several wars fought between Denmark and the Baltic Sea states.

Second union with Sweden

During the reign of Napoleon, Denmark was allied with France, so when Napoleon's rule in Europe came to an end, the Danes were forced to cede control of Norway to the powerful nearby Swedes. However, Norway had hopes of emerging from these troubles as an independent state: on 17 May 1814 (now a pub-

The Hanseatic Museum in Bryggen, Bergen contains an authentic trading room from the early 18th century.

lic holiday), the country declared itself an autonomous kingdom and approved a constitution. However, pressure from Stockholm forced Norway to abandon its plans, and it was annexed by Sweden, ending over 400 years of union between the Danes and the Norwegians. In return, Stock-holm recognized Norway's constitution and allowed the country to govern itself within the framework of a union led by Sweden. Despite this increase of political influence, Norway suffered greatly from its split with Denmark over subsequent years, being cut off from its trade and industry. Following the British market embargo on Norwegian wood, the sawmills lost many foreign customers, and the economic crisis also affected the Norwegian middle class with countless businesses going bankrupt. The revolutionary ideas emerging in many European countries in 1848 also began to surface in Norway, but these nationalistic leanings were not limited to the political sphere but rather also encompassed intellectual life, which from this point on was characterized by a renaissance of national culture. The pursuit of independence was becoming unstoppable. In 1905, Norway dissolved the union with Sweden by a parliamentary consensus and a referendum, called for by Stockholm, and the Parliament elected Haakon VII as king of Norway.

An autonomous kingdom

Norway reconnected with its seafaring heritage and expanded its merchant navy. The country's economic recovery was matched by an outbreak of "America fever", and hundreds of thousands of Norwegians emigrated to North America. However, at the same time Norwegian polar explorers were creating a sensation. By the end of the 19th century, Fridtjof Nansen had already made several successful expeditions into the Arctic, paving the way for Roald Amundsen to become the first man to reach the South Pole in 1911.

Norway was able to remain neutral during World War I. However, its reliance on foreign trade meant that it was hit hard by the worldwide economic crisis of 1929. When World War II broke out, Norway remained a neutral power, but its later occupation by German forces in 1940 forced the king and his cabinet to flee to London, which became the home of Norway's government in exile over the following years. After the war had ended, Haakon VII was finally able to return home.

Modern Norway

Norway renounced its traditional neutrality in 1949 by becoming a member of NATO and membership of the European Free Trade Association (EFTA) in 1960 brought the country increased opportunity for trade. Norway, unlike nearby Sweden, Finland, and Denmark, has still not joined the European Union. In 1970 the government formally applied for acceptance into the EU (at the time called the European Economic Community), but this request was rescinded in 1972 following a referendum. Norwegians reasserted their nationalism once again in a 1994 referendum voting against EU membership. Opponents of membership are mindful of the independence and national identity of a country that has also grown economically strong due to an abundance of crude oil and natural gas, while its supporters warn of the dangers of political isolation. Nevertheless, Norway plays a prominent role in international diplomacy.

Wooden houses form the distinctive landscape of the "mountain town" of Røros, which was a copper-mining site between 1644 and 1977.

King Haakon VII escaped to exile in Britain in 1940.

Norway is rich in natural oil fields, and all the major international oil companies have a presence in Stavanger.

PROFILE: MIDNIGHT SUN AND THE NORTHERN LIGHTS

World-famous Norwegians in the arts (from left): The painter Edvard Munch (1863–1944) was a pioneer of expressionism; Henrik Ibsen (1828–1906) is regarded as the creator of modern drama; Nobel Laureate Bjørnstjerne Bjørnson (1832–1910) composed the words to the Norwegian national anthem; Knut Hamsun (1859–1952) was awarded a Nobel Prize for his novel *Growth of the Soil*; Edvard Grieg (1843–1907) was a composer inspired by Norway's folk music; Liv Ullmann (b. 1938) is an actress and director.

Edvard Munch

Scandinavia's most influential painter is counted as one of the pioneers of European expressionism. Edvard Munch (1863–1944) took inspiration from the expressionists during his time in Paris. His art is characterized by vivid, stark contrasts, and many of his paintings focus on elementary themes such

Emotion in the raw: *Anxiety* (1894).

as anxiety, hopelessness, loneliness, and death. Munch, who also spent a period of time in Germany, weaved expressions of the darker side of human existence (a side he well knew) into his work, notably the celebrated 1893 painting *The Scream*. During later periods of his creative life, the Norwegian landscape became a recurring motif. The artist bequeathed his estate to the capital city of Oslo, where many of his works are displayed in the Munch Museum, as well as in the National Gallery.

The establishment of a Norwegian literary identity

Old Norwegian literature has close links with Old Icelandic and post-15th-century Danish poetry. It was only after the split from Denmark that Norway's own independent strand of national literature began to emerge. Henrik Ibsen (1828–1906) is considered to be the father of modern drama whose plays are dissections of society and portray existential conflicts with an expert hand. Plays such as *Peer Gynt* (1867), *A Doll's House* (1879), *Ghosts* (1881), and *The Master Builder* (1892) brought him worldwide renown. Various Norwegian authors including the equally politically minded Bjørnstjerne Bjørnson (1832–1910), Knut Hamsun (1859–1952), whose work is characterized by a distinctive distaste for civilization, and Sigrid Undset (1882–1949), many of whose plays were set in the Middle Ages, have been awarded the Nobel Prize in Literature.

Folk music, classical music, and jazz

The Hardanger fiddle (a violin with four or five strings) is one of the most important instruments in Norwegian folk music, along with a variety of other instruments steeped in tradition: the Jew's harp, the goat horn, various flutes, and the Norwegian zither. Folk tunes played on these instruments have inspired many different composers, most notably Edvard Grieg (1843–1907), who heralded the "golden age" of Norwegian music. He aspired

above all to give music a national form of expression, and so wove old folk tunes into modern compositional forms. Grieg's chamber and orchestral works brought him worldwide renown, along with his incidental music – for instance, his score for Ibsen's play *Peer Gynt*, commissioned by the playwright himself. Norway plays host to many music festivals, one of the most popular being the Bergen International Festival, established in 1953. Other tourist attractions include the Oslo Contemporary Music Festival, the Festival of North Norway, and the jazz festivals in Molde and Kongsberg.

Award-winning architecture

Norway's medieval stave churches are the most

Rose painting inside the medieval chapel in Heddal, the largest stave church of its kind in Norway.

The Hardanger fiddle is not only heard in folk music – it also makes appearances in classical concerts.

famous symbol of the country's architecture, and represent an important contribution to the world's architectural heritage – Urnes' particularly ornamental stave church was designated a UNESCO World Heritage Site in 1979. The very same year, this distinction was also granted to Bergen's waterfront area of Bryggen, a collection of hundreds of wooden houses. This

Expert woodcarving

In a densely wooded country such as Norway, wood is understandably a very important resource. Whilst early settlers used it for construction and fuel, later inhabitants also used it for decoration. Some of the earliest examples of Norwegian indigenous woodcarving are the ornately carved wooden Viking ships, regarded as

sacred buildings. Hundreds of so-called stave churches were built, mostly during the 12th and 13th centuries. Now only a few dozen remain, and are counted among the oldest wooden structures in the world. These churches take their name from the wooden posts and beams that form a network of multilevel, tiered beams to create the building's framework.

Arts and crafts

One decorative technique commonly used in Norway is that of rose painting (Rosemaling), a form of rural art. Its title is somewhat misleading, as roses are merely one of the many images depicted in this typically Norwegian folk art. Originating in the east of the country in the mid-18th century, it is used to decorate everyday household

Magical: carvings in Gol stave church.

Oslo Opera House, which was immediately adopted as the new emblem of Norway's capital, opened in April 2008 with a performance of Wagner's *The Flying Dutchman*.

area, already established in the 13th century, has burnt down many times but was rebuilt in its original form on each occasion.
Norway is even setting trends in modern architecture, the most recent example being the National Opera House, Oslo's newest landmark. This futuristic-looking, marble-clad building, designed by architecture firm Snøhetta, is intended' to symbolize an iceberg rising from the sea. Praised for its scale, ambition, and quality, at the Barcelona World Architecture Festival it was named World Cultural Building of the year.

masterpieces of early medieval carpentry. These exceptionally seaworthy vessels, strong even in rough conditions but equally at home in inland waterways, were decorated with particularly artistic carved dragon heads, earning them the name "dragon boats".
The Vikings were equally adept at carving as a way of manufacturing basic commodities, which (like the beams in their houses) were often also ornately decorated. The growth of Christianity in Norway gave woodcarvers new opportunities in the adornment of

Stave churches were common in northern Europe at one time and traces of them are still to be found in Denmark, Sweden, and Germany. Several replicas have been built in other countries, including in the United States, such as the Hopperstad replica stave church in Moorhead, Minnesota.
Wooden houses, as well as sacred buildings, were also delicately carved, with the entrances and window frames in particular boasting decoration unique to each building. This tradition continues to this day, with many wooden houses still displaying ornate carvings.

objects, doors, and furniture, using flowing lines, scrolls, and elaborate flourishes (as well as roses), often painted in vivid colors. The relative isolation of many parts of Norway, and thus the lack of contact between different areas, led to the development of various styles and techniques. The 19th century saw the emergence of glassworks and porcelain factories, producing both everyday goods and a variety of valuable art pieces. Norway continues to produce notable examples of glassware and pottery, along with delicate pieces of local gold and silverware.

Each region of Norway has its own particular traditional dress. Today, around three-quarters of all Norwegians still own a traditional folk costume, even though a complete outfit with all the accompanying accessories is likely to cost more than 1,000 Euros. These decorative costumes are chiefly worn on 17 May (Norway's Constitution Day) when the streets are filled with people celebrating together.

Trolls

Norway has a rich tradition of myths, legends, fables, and fantasies. There are stories of trolls living in the mountains to the north, where gnarled trees cast long shadows and secluded forest lakes glisten in the moonlight. Sinister beings with withered hair and shining eyes, they spend their nights playing all kinds of practical jokes on trav-

These comical trolls can be found almost everywhere.

elers. According to legend, these trolls can be towering or tiny, even having different numbers of heads or eyes. However, despite their fearsome appearance, trolls are good-natured – at least most are, as long as no one angers them... Visitors who fail to see a real troll can be consoled with the huge range of weird and comical likenesses, in all shapes and sizes, which are sold in the souvenir shops everywhere.

The value of accessible education

Norway, like the other Scandinavian countries, prides itself on its high educational standards, a fact regularly proven in international comparisons. For example, even people living in the remote areas of Norway have an excellent command of English, as it is taught from the very beginning of primary school. The country's culture and society has long been geared toward the Anglo-Saxon world, and the creation of equal opportunities for all citizens is the foundation of its education policy. School syllabuses are laid down by the state, and compulsory education lasts for ten years. All forms of public education are free. Even far outside the largest cities, there is a remarkable basic level of cultural activity, and throughout Norway people are very welcoming of the advances of modern times.

A different kettle of fish

Norway is not commonly considered a stronghold of gastronomy, but this stereotype does a disservice to the country's quality of food – in 2009 Norwegian chef Geir Skeie was awarded the gold medal in the prestigious international cookery competition, the Bocuse d'Or.
One of the country's natural treasures is its marine world, boasting a huge number and variety of species. Fish and related products are not only important exports – they are also traditionally used in home cooking, in a huge variety of ways. Stockfish (dried

whitefish) has been exported almost from time immemorial, and the culture surrounding the drying of fish in Norway can be traced back centuries. *Lutefisk* (lye fish) – dried fish soaked in lye and then boiled, served with potatoes and pease pudding – is a very popular dish during Advent and at Christmas. *Fiskeboller* (little fish balls) or *fiskepudding* (in effect a Norwegian meal of leftovers) are simple, but very popular dishes. Moving from traditional cooking to rarefied

An impressive array of stockfish: shops such as this one in the fishing village of Reine in the Lofoten Islands, are an indication that fish features heavily in many restaurant menus.

cuisine, skrei is without a doubt becoming an essential ingredient in any ambitious menu. This delicacy, also known as winter cod, migrates during the coldest part of the year from the Barents Sea to the Lofoten Islands, where the fishermen hungrily await them.

The origins of skiing

Norway's abundant winter snow offers prime conditions for skiing. Evidence has been found of skis already being

used for transport around 4,000 years ago. In the middle of the 19th century, this tradition was given an unexpected boost by the pioneering Sondre Nordheim, from the Telemark region, who developed fixed ski bindings, which made jumps and turns possible. Nordheim is regarded as the founder of slalom skiing, which takes its name from the Norwegian words *sla* (slope) and *låm* (tracks).
Norwegian polar explorers took advantage of this

method of crossing snow while on their expeditions – Fridtjof Nansen, when exploring Greenland, and Roald Amundsen on his Antarctic trek, both covered large distances on skis. Today, skiing is still Norway's best-loved sport, and the Holmenkollen ski jump, near Oslo, is the Mecca of Nordic skiing. During high-ranking international competitions, crowds of spectators flood in. The Winter Olympics have already been held in Norway twice:

Oslo in 1952 and Lillehammer in 1994.

Midsummer Night

This is a unique night in the
calendar. As the beginning of
summer draws closer and the
threshold between day and
night gradually dwindles, an
atmosphere of anticipation
pervades the whole country.
All over Norway, the night of
the summer solstice at the end
of June heralds the traditional
Midsummer Night celebra-
tions. Even if it is only the
northern third of the country
that experiences the glow of
the sun the whole night long,
every little town south of the
Arctic Circle still dances and
celebrates. Enormous bonfires
are lit, and the mood is very
lively. This Norwegian tradition dates back as long as
anyone can remember. The
various Midsummer Night
festivities that take place in
coastal areas include the taking of fire to the offshore
islands by boat. According to
ancient tradition, it will help
drive away evil spirits. Midsummer Night is represented
in every form of art, explored
by painters, composers, actors,
and authors alike.

Bokmål and *Nynorsk*: two languages co-existing

Norwegian is a Germanic
language. It consists of two
strains, *Bokmål* (book language) and *Nynorsk* (New
Norwegian). Bokmål, the
older language, contains
structures and a vocabulary
heavily derived from Danish,
and was Norway's official
language for centuries. During Danish rule, however,

Ablaze: at Laerdalsøyri, Sognefjord, Midsummer Night celebrations are hotting up.

This folk dance troupe gives a convincing performance in a traditional dance of celebration at the Norsk Folkemuseum (Norwegian Museum of Cultural History) on the Bygdøy penin-sula in the Oslofjord.

the rural dialects developed
and evolved. It was only after
the end of more than 400
years of union with Denmark
in 1814 that the pronuncia-
tion and grammar of Bokmål
really became "Norwegian".
To match the increasing
national consciousness, the
19th century saw increasing
calls by Norwegians for their
"own" language free from
any aspects of Danish. This
saw the birth of Nynorsk,
based on Norwegian dialects,
which was recognized as a
second official written lan-

guage in 1885. The languages
coexist and see equal use in
the official arena (in the
media, in schools, and in
administration). Each local
community chooses which
language will be used in its
schools, but pupils are also
taught the alternative language, as secondary schools
require both. Bokmål is much
more widespread, whilst
Nynorsk (predominantly spoken in rural areas) has never
really been able to gain a
foothold in the political and
economical arena.

Nouns are classified by gender,
as with most Indo-European
languages, and Norwegian has
three genders: masculine,
feminine, and neuter. The
majority of the Norwegian
vocabulary is derived from
Old Norse, but aside from
that, many words come from
Middle Low German, which
was spoken from around
1100 to 1600. These days,
most new words to enter the
language come from English,
though Norwegian is less
influenced by English than
say are Swedish and Danish.

THE HIGHLIGHTS

VESTLANDET

As the name suggests, Vestlandet lies in the western part of Norway and is the country's number one tourist destination, containing the most spectacular fjords, the biggest glaciers in mainland Europe, and several national parks. The majority of the country's stave churches are here, as well as four UNESCO World Heritage Sites: Urnes stave church in the Lustrafjord, the Hanseatic district of Bryggen in Bergen, the Geirangerfjord, and Nærøyfjord. The city of Stavanger combines old and new, with Norway's oldest cathedral and a NATO base.

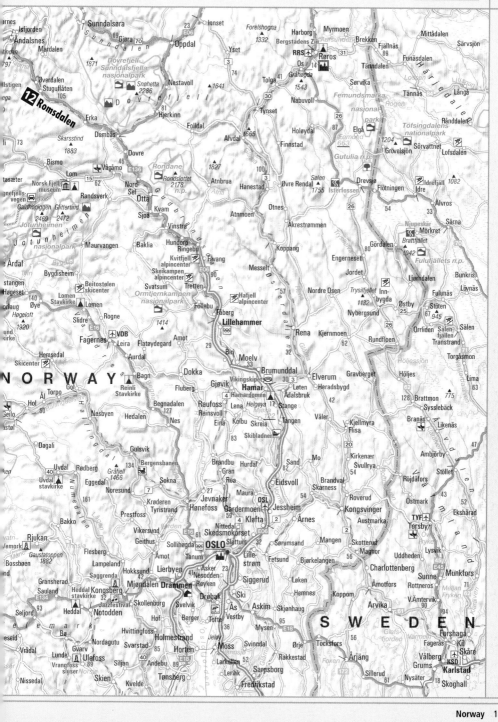

THE HIGHLIGHTS: VESTLANDET

The old district of Gamle Stavanger, containing more than 150 wooden houses from the 18th and 19th centuries (below), represents a complete, intact collection of this style of building – a global rarity. The Romanesque Cathedral rises above the lake, Breiavatnet (right). Inset below: A view over the port.

TIP Sørensens restaurant

This unique restaurant's full name is Sørensens Dampskibsexpedition. The walls are covered from floor to ceiling in souvenirs. The cuisine is light and imaginative.
Skagen 26, 4006 Stavanger; Tel 51 84 38 20; Mon–Wed 11.00–24.00, Thurs–Sat 11.00–2.00, Sun 13.00–24.00.

Stavanger, in the Boknafjord, is the capital of Rogaland province. It was here that King Harald Hårfagre (Fairhair) united the separate Norwegian kingdoms in 872, a fact commemorated in the Hafrsfjord by some enormous sculptures of Viking swords. The Romanesque cathedral (completed in 1125) is considered one of Norway's best preserved medieval places of worship built in stone. The Norsk Hermetikkmuseum (Norwegian Canning Museum) documents the business of a former factory in a branch of industry that left its mark on the life of the town from the 1840s: in the middle of the 20th century there were 50 sardine canning factories here, with the final factory only closing in 2002. Even Stavanger's rapid rise as a base for the crude oil and natural gas industries (from 1971 onward) has not dented the city's traditions: the restored old wooden district of Gamle Stavanger is a protected conservation area. (See also pp. 160, 178.)

Research into techniques for extracting offshore natural resources, along with the production of much of the necessary equipment (right and inset below), plays a central role in Stavanger. A decrease in pressure has caused the seabed in the Ekofisk oil field to drop 7 m (23 feet), and so the construction of a new platform (below) took into account a drop in ground level of 20 m (66 feet).

BLACK GOLD: OFFSHORE RICHES

The coastal city of Stavanger is the crude oil and natural gas capital of Norway. The national oil company Statoil has a presence here, along with other international oil firms, and the nearby airport in Sola is a hub for all traffic to the North Sea oil rigs. When the Ekofisk oil field was opened around 300 km (186 miles) offshore in 1971, it heralded the beginning of the Norwegian North Sea base's offshore oil production, supplemented in 1977 by the extraction of natural gas. Since then, the extraction, production, transportation, and marketing of oil and natural gas have become Norway's most important branch of industry, and have left their mark particularly on Stavanger's development and cityscape. The Ekofisk oil field, numbering 29 offshore installations, is the biggest industrial zone in the North Sea, and has long been a junction for piping toward the continent of Europe. At the beginning of 2005, 440 million tons of the 524.1 million tons of oil originally discovered had already been extracted; the extraction licence runs until 2028. Stavanger also plays a vital role in research, as the extraction of crude oil and natural gas are by no means without their problems: in 1977, there was a nine-day-long "blowout" of an oil and gas composite, which covered more than 55,000 sq. km (22,200 sq. miles) of the ocean's surface in a few weeks. Three years later, the accommodation rig "Alexander Kjelland" capsized in a storm, killing 123 people.

THE HIGHLIGHTS:
VESTLANDET

INFO Vintage ship

The stone "pulpit" of Prekestolen, standing almost 600 m (1,970 feet) high with sheer drops on three sides (right and below), offers a sweeping view across the Lysefjord as far as the mountain landscape of Ryfylkeheiene, and of Kjerag's impressive sheer rock faces rising some 1,000 m (3,280 feet) above the ground. Below right: Kjerag's wedged boulder.

During the summer, the venerable old ship the MS *Riskafjord II* (built in 1864) makes daily crossings of the Lysefjord. The two-hour-long journey from Høle, across the middle of the Lysefjord to Prekestolen and back again, features fantastic views.
4395 Hommersåk; Tel 51 67 10 00.
www.riskafjord.no

To the east of Stavanger, the Lysefjord carves its way around 40 km (25 miles) through the mountain landscape of Ryfylkeheiene and offers thrilling scenery, including the Kerag where a huge boulder is wedged between two sheer rock walls, and Prekestolen ("Pulpit Rock") where a flat ledge above a massive cliff face offers heartstopping, but unprotected (be warned) views. Visitors wanting to play it safe and gaze up at it from below can take a boat down the Lysefjord: the ferry leaves Forsand at the fjord's mouth for Lysebotn, from where a spectacular road snakes its way across the landscape. The Lysefjordsenteret (tourist information office) in Oanes, situated on the Riksveg (literally, "road of the realm") bridge over the mouth of the fjord, has information on all there is to know about the popular Lysefjord and its surrounding mountain scenery, and provides details of walks and climbing sites.

INFO Folk museum

The Låtefossen waterfall in Odda plummets 165 m (541 feet) down through the south-western foothills of the Hardangervidda (below and far right). The legendary Riksveg 13 (far right, bottom) crosses the lower part of the waterfall by means of an arched bridge. Right: Island life in the Hardangerfjord.

A typical Hardanger farm was reconstructed especially for this open-air museum of folk culture. There is also a historic shop and a range of traditional Hardranger ships.

5778 Utne; Tel 53 67 00 40; Sept–Apr Mon–Sat 10.00–15.00, May–Jun 10.00–16.00 daily, Jul–Aug, 10.00–18.00 daily.

At over 150 km (93 miles) long, the spectacular Hardangerfjord presides over a collection of smaller inlets. Its sprawling network of tributary fjords stretches from the island landscape of the south-west to the foothills of the Hardangervidda, the largest high mountain plateau in northern Europe, which has been designated a national park. The fjords branching off to the north-east surround the Folgefonna peninsula, a towering glacial mountain landscape that has also been awarded the protected status of national park. The higher areas boast peaks, ski slopes, and glaciers, while lower altitudes feature cherry blossom and sun-kissed water-side areas; the Hardanger region, offering some of Norway's most diverse scenery, also takes great care to conserve a culture that has evolved over many centuries, its folk costumes (Hardanger embroidery) and music (the Hardanger fiddle and traditional dancing) earning particular renown.

THE HIGHLIGHTS: VESTLANDET

INFO Glacier tours

In search of a lost era: the Kaiservegen ("Emperor's Way", right), laid down in the 1890s, is a spectacular way of climbing the breathtaking glacial landscape of Folgefonna (below), offering a superb view that changes constantly in the play of the light according to the time of day.

By the 19th century, visitors were already using the Sundalsvegen to cross the Folgefonna glacier. The old trails have now been repaired and transformed into accessible paths, and are used by hiking groups led by experienced guides. *Folgefonni Breførarlag, 5627 Jondal; Tel 55 29 89 21.*

In May 2005, Queen Sonja opened Norway's 25th national park, which covers around 545 sq. km (210 sq. miles) and includes the third largest glacier in Scandinavia. The plateau glacier, reaching up to 34 km (21 miles) in length and as much as 16 km (10 miles) across in some places, is on the Folgefonna penin-sula, enclosed by the Sør and other branches of the Hardangerfjord. The national park is marked by fjells, glaciers, lakes, cirques, and fertile valleys boasting a variety of deciduous woodland, as well as mountain streams, and lakes rich in trout and salmon. The peninsula has long been a troublesome obstacle for drivers, but the opening of the Folgefonna Tunnel in 2001, stretching 11,500 m (37,700 feet) through the 1,662-m (5,453-foot) high mountain range between Odda on the Sørfjord and Gjerde on the Maurangerfjord, makes negotiating it much easier. It used to take four hours but now takes ten minutes.

THE HIGHLIGHTS: VESTLANDET

INFO Handcar trips

The legendary Hårteigen, towering 1,690 m (5,545 feet) over the western part of the plateau, is the most striking mountain on the Hardangervidda (right). Around the national park, many alpine valleys have been converted into reservoirs. Below: The Trolltunga precipice jutting out over the lake, known as Ringedalsvatnet.

Far away from urban areas, handcars are a comfortable way of getting around using the disused Rjukan rail line running through the beautiful countryside. At Mæl station, Rjukanbanen vehicles can be hired for excursions.
Tourist information: Tinnsjø Kro, 3658 Miland; Tel 35 09 05 85.

Hardangervidda is the largest high mountain plain in northern Europe, whose 3,422 sq. km (1,321 sq. miles) have been designated a national park since 1981. To the west, the ground falls away in a 1,000-m (3,280-foot) high escarpment leading down to the Sørfjord, and to the east it tapers gently into the valleys of Østlandet. This marshy plateau of gneiss and granite is home to Europe's largest population of wild reindeer, and its polar climate makes it one of the most southerly places to see polar wildlife such as snowy owls and Arctic foxes. Snow and ice remain right into the summer months, even though the highest peak of Sandfloeggi, capped with residual ice, is only 1,719 m (5,640 feet) high. Trails head toward Hårteigen from all directions, granting a terrific panorama across the Vidda toward Gausta in the south-west, the Folgefonna glacier to the west, and the Hardangerjøkulen in the north-east.

THE HIGHLIGHTS: VESTLANDET

TIP Bryggen Tracteursted

Composer Edvard Grieg (1843–1907) is the most famous Norwegian to have come from Bergen (inset below). In 1885 he built the nearby Troldhaugen villa, now open to the public as a museum (right). A magical evening atmosphere illuminates the waterfront (below), but Bergen's marketplace is bustling with life (below right).

An interesting contrast: visitors will enjoy this restaurant's modern, locally inspired cuisine, which is served in the historic ambience of a 200-year-old assembly room in Bergen's historical Hanseatic district. *Bryggestredet 2, 5019 Bergen; Tel 55 33 69 99; May–Sept from 11.00 daily, Oct–Apr Tues–Sat from 17.00.*

This university port on the Byfjord is Norway's second most important economic and cultural city after Oslo, and the second biggest city in the country with around 237,000 inhabitants. The city is set among seven mountains and has an international seaport catering for both container and cruise ships.

Bergen's marketplace is one of the most vibrant and famous in the whole of Scandinavia. Before the opening of the Bergen Line in 1909, the city could be reached more quickly from London than from Oslo. Since there are no natural routes leading inland, for centuries Bergen's contact with the rest of the

world was by sea. Bergen's festival has also earned it international renown: every year at the end of May and beginning of June, tens of thousands of visitors from all over the world flock to the city to enjoy the sights and entertainments of the Festspillene i Bergen. (See also pp. 161, 180.)

The cog was the main vessel used for transporting Hanseatic goods (right). Reconstructions of these cargo ships, found on the waterfront in the Hanseatic district of Bryggen, are a protected part of the World Heritage Site. The houses belonging to merchants designed for ease of loading and unloading ships, stand right on the dock (below).

BRYGGEN HANSEATIC DISTRICT

Bryggeloftet & stuene

The Hanseatic district of Bryggen in Bergen, once known as Tyskebryggen ("German bridges") because it acted as a base for the German merchants of the Hanseatic League, was added to the list of UNESCO World Heritage Sites in 1979. This area of painted wooden houses in the old port has been reconstructed following several catastrophic fires. In the passageways between merchants' houses and warehouses there is an aroma of wood and tar, and various winches and hooks protrude from hatches that were used to unload "Bergen fish" (stockfish), blubber, hides, beer, wine, and salt, as well as swords, armor, and textiles over the course of at least half a millennium. The historic port houses various reconstructed cogs, small sailing vessels used for transporting goods to Hanseatic cities in Germany, England, Flanders, and the Baltic provinces. The Hanseatic Museum, situated in the Finnegård merchant's house, provides information for visitors on the Hanseatic League, an association of merchants. This trading, logistic, and colonization organization was hugely powerful in central and northern Europe during the late Middle Ages. It came into being during the 12th century as an informal syndicate among business proprietors who wanted to reap the economic rewards of cooperation. Members were afforded protection from pirates and robber barons. By the late 16th century the League was in decline; it was dissolved in 1862.

The voyage from Bergen to Kirkenes: the Hurtigruten voyage is most rewarding at the height of summer, when night becomes day. Tickets for winter trips are comparatively inexpensive, but have their own attractions: the Northern Lights glow in the sky, you are not jostled by crowds of people on board, and the ports are aglow with a welcoming blaze of light.

HURTIGRUTE: THE WORLD'S MOST BEAUTIFUL SEA VOYAGE

Every evening at 20.00, a Hurtigruten ferry sets off from the Hanseatic city of Bergen and negotiates the Hjeltefjord, along which the Vikings once journeyed on their way to the Shetland Islands. The voyage, 2,500 nautical miles in length and lasting a total of 12 days, travels from Bergen to Kirkenes on the northern Norwegian border with Russia, and back again. The Gulf Stream ensures that the country's ports remain free of ice the whole year round. Both the outward and return journeys are designed to make sure that passengers miss nothing of the spectacular coastal landscape as it appears by day and night: the ports that are only seen under cover of darkness during the voyage northward, appear bustling and active on the return journey during the day. Even though a few of the older mailboats are still in action, the Hurtigrute route established in 1893 as a cargo and postal delivery service is now little more than a tourist attraction. There are three distinct types of ship: the so-called traditional vessels dating from the 1950s and 1960s, the more comfortable versions dating from 1982–83, and the luxurious "new generation" vessels. By 2006 there were already 14 ships in general use, all with one important point in common: none of them put on shows, have Muzak playing in the background, or hold discos or entertainment of any kind. Passengers are invited simply to experience the scenery – one of the most beautiful landscapes on this earth.

THE HIGHLIGHTS: VESTLANDET

At a good 24 km (15 miles) long, this is easily the longest road tunnel in the world: the Lærdal Tunnel (inset below, top) has replaced the car ferries on the Aurlandsfjord (below, right), a branch of the Sognefjord. Borgund stave church (built around 1150) is one of Norway's most beautiful (right).

INFO Stave church, Borgund

Borgund's stave church, at around 900 years old, is regarded as the best preserved example in Norway. An exhibition attached to the church explains the background history behind this type of building, and displays similar archeological finds.
Tel 57 66 81 09; 18 May–14 Sept 10.00–17.00, 11 Jun–21 Aug 8.00–20.00.

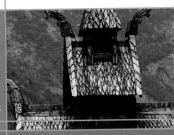

At 204 km (127 miles) long, Sognefjord is the longest fjord in Europe, and the deepest in the world, reaching down to 1,308 m (4,291 feet) below sea level in places. A popular destination for international cruises and for the Hurtigruten ships in the summer months, which travel along this natural waterway cutting deep into the mountain landscape, is the branch that narrows down to a mere 250 m (820 feet) across, the Nærøyfjord in Aurland; it is flanked by rock faces up to 1,800 m (5,900 feet) high, and its natural beauty merited its inclusion on the list of UNESCO World Heritage Sites in 2005. The Urnes stave church, also awarded this distinction, stands at the innermost end of the fjord immediately adjacent to the highest mountain in Scandinavia. The 12th-century stave church in Borgund can be found at the foot of this imposing mountain landscape in the meadows of Lærdal, one of the valleys running from the Sognefjord toward Fillefjell.

INFO Sognefjell road

Vikings, by now Christianized, would cross the Lustrafjord in order to pray in the stave church (right and below) on the Urnes headland. Modern reconstructions have altered its original form, but the sumptuous decorative carvings (below right) remain intact.

The pass between Sognefjord and Gudbrandstal has been opened up to traffic as a Green Route. This stretch of road runs for some 110 km (68 miles) across the highest pass in northern Europe.

Statens vegvesen; Tel 81 52 20 00.
www.turistveg.no

Urnes is home to Norway's oldest remaining stave church. It was erected in 1130 among majestic natural scenery on what was (and still is) a relatively isolated headland in the Lustrafjord, the most inland branch of the Sognefjord. This place of worship has been a protected UNESCO World Heritage Site since 1979. The church's construction and layout appear perfect, a fact explained only by the country's long tradition of local wooden architecture in the building of farms and boats. The most artistically and culturally significant elements of the church are without a doubt the carvings, found in the nave and choir on the cushion capitals of the "staves" (pillars or poles), in the north entrance, and on the northern wall. This ornamentation is characteristic of Urnes style, and is also found on rune stones and silver jewelry originating from the area once inhabited by the Vikings that stretches from Denmark to the border with Lapland.

THE HIGHLIGHTS: VESTLANDET

The Jostedalsbreen and its surrounding area have had protected national park status (below) since 1991. The park office and museum can be found in the Breheimsenteret (tourist information office), based on a design inspired by a glacial crevasse, which is the starting point for expertly led hikes on the glacier (right).

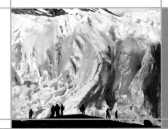

Situated at the entrance to the Jostedalsbreen National Park, this ultra-modern tourist information office also has an interesting museum.

Breheimsenteret, 6871 Jostedal; Tel 57 68 32 50; 1 May–30 Sept 9.00–19.00 daily, before Jun 21 and from Aug 20 10.00–17.00

he Jostedalsbreen (Jostedal glacier) is ꭇe biggest in continental Europe. The ꟷateau glacier, measuring up to 15 km Ꭵ miles) across, stretches from the ꭒland branches of the Sognefjord 100 ꭑ (62 miles) toward the north-east. In ꬲme places, the ice is up to 500 m Ꮪ,640 feet) thick. The Høgste Breakulen is a 1,957-m (6,421-foot) mountain peak, covered in ice and the highest point on the glacier. A few other rocky peaks jut out here and there from the ice mass, the tallest being Lodalskåpa (2,083 m/6,834 feet). The glacier's branches sprawl down into many of the valleys of Jostedalen, which is 50 km (31 miles) long, and can be reached by road. The most famous branch, the Brigsdalsbreen, is situated on the sunnier north-western side of the Jostedals-breen. The main winter highlight is the Nigardsbreen Ice Cave and Blue Lagoon. The glacier has been gradually retreating for the last 200 years.

THE HIGHLIGHTS: VESTLANDET

INFO Eagle Way

The panoramic Dalsnibba (1,476 m/ 4,843 feet high), which can be reached by car along a 5-km (3-mile) toll road, offers a majestic view across the weird mountain world of Sunnmøre (below), sliced in two by the powerful Geirangerfjord (right, with the Seven Sisters waterfall), which reaches depths of more than 1,000 m (3,280 feet).

The Ørneveien ("Eagle Way") to Geiranger can only be described in superlatives. Its winding bends offer a world-famous, magnificent view of the fjord and the waterfalls on its banks. From the north, the Ørneveien is approached by way of Ålesund or the Trollstigvegen from Åndalsnes.

The Geirangerfjord, one of the world's most beautiful stretches of scenery, has been a UNESCO World Heritage Site since 2005. It is the innermost branch of the 120-km (75-mile) long Storfjord, which every year plays host to more than 150 cruise ships from all over the world. Gazing out from the ships, the view boasts among other things three famous waterfalls: the Seven Sisters, the Friar, and the Bridal Veil. In the summer, the Hurtigruten ships make berth in Geiranger at the end of the fjord, a tiny village with only 250 inhabitants. The Ørneveien (Eagle Way), a mountain road that stretches north from Geirangerfjord to the Norddalsfjord, with its winding route and observation points, is one of the most breathtaking mountain passes in the whole of Scandinavia. The most spectacular observation point is only accessible on foot: the 112-m (367-foot) high Flydalshornet, lying perpendicular to the fjord.

THE HIGHLIGHTS: VESTLANDET

TIP Sjøbua restaurant

The Ålesund boat museum (inset below) documents the maritime history of the coastal town (right), rebuilt in 1904 following a fire. The best panoramic view can be found by climbing the 418 steps from the town park up to the top of Aksla (below).

The historic warehouse on the waterfront in Ålesund is home to one of Norway's best fish restaurants, where fish from the daily catch – or lobsters from the in-house salt-water tank – are prepared according to local tradition. *Brunholmsgt, 1A, 6004 Ålesund; Tel 70 12 71 00; Mon–Fri 16.00–1.00.*

A small town extending across three islands at the mouth of the Storfjord, Ålesund is the principal town of the Sunnmøre region and Norway's largest fishing port. With its art nouveau architectural style, the town is unique in all of Norway. However, Ålesund is principally known for its centuries-old export trade of *klippfisk* ("cliff fish"): The fishermen would salt their catch, mostly different varieties of cod, and dry it on the cliffs along the coastline – hence the name. The islands off the coast shelter the town and port from the open sea. Runde is the most famous island in the Sørøyane Archipelago, granted protected status for its bird population. Every year, the towering, sheer cliffs become a heavily populated breeding ground for up to 700,000 seabirds, including a colony of 5,000 pairs of fulmars. It is possible to travel by boat between Åndalsnes and Runde. (See also p. 161.)

INFO Unusual chapel

Views across the Romsdalsalpene (right) and over the Trollstigen, the most famous serpentine road in Scandinavia (below). This "Troll Ladder" begins at sea level in the port of Åndalsnes (below right), where it leaves Romsdalen and curves upwards in a series of hairpin bends to a height of 870 m (2,850 feet).

The final station of the Rauma Line in Åndalsnes is home to the "church on rails", probably the only such example in the world. This unusual place of worship is an old train carriage, opened in 2003 by the king and queen of Norway.
Jernbanestasjonen,
6300 Åndalsnes; Tel 71 22 16 22.

This unique valley is known as Romsdalen. Along with the Romsdalsalpene mountain range, it forms one of the most spectacular coastal and mountain landscapes in all of Norway. The Rauma River flows down through the valley from Dovrefjell and into the port of Åndalsnes along the many branches of the Romsdalfjord, where the Romsdalen continues submerged under water. The high mountains on both sides, covered with expanses of ice, rise up around 1,800 m (5,900 feet). Some of the area's famous landmarks include the Trolltindan mountain peaks, their tips towering more than 1,700 m (5,600 feet) above the bottom of the valley, and the 1,000-m (3,280-foot) high Trollveggen rock face. The valley is accessible by car along European route E136, and by a beautiful scenic railway: the 114km (71-mile) Raumabanen (Rauma Line) route leads from Dombås to Åndalsnes though a breathtaking mountain landscape.

THE HIGHLIGHTS

ØSTLANDET

Østlandet is situated in the eastern part of Norway and extends from Oslo, the green capital city on the Oslofjord, to Jotunheimen National Park, where the highest peaks in northern Europe are to be found, and from Telemark, acknowledged as the birthplace of skiing, to the abundant lakes and ancient forests of the national parks on the Swedish border. Lillehammer, the unofficial world capital of winter sport, nestles between Mjøsa, Norway's largest lake, and Gudbrandsdalen, Norway's "valley of valleys".

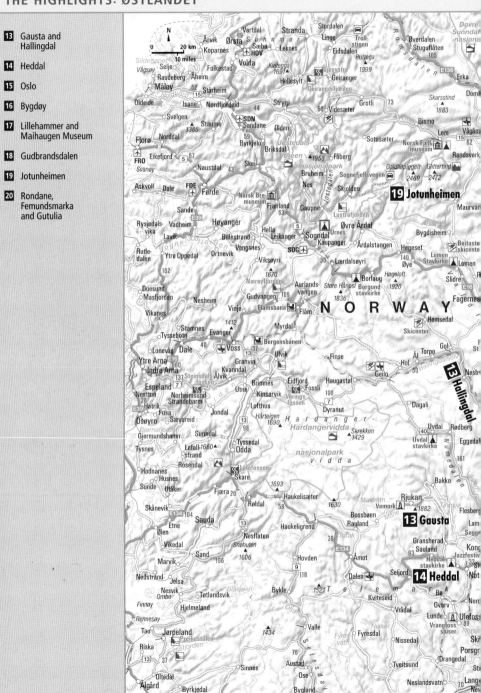

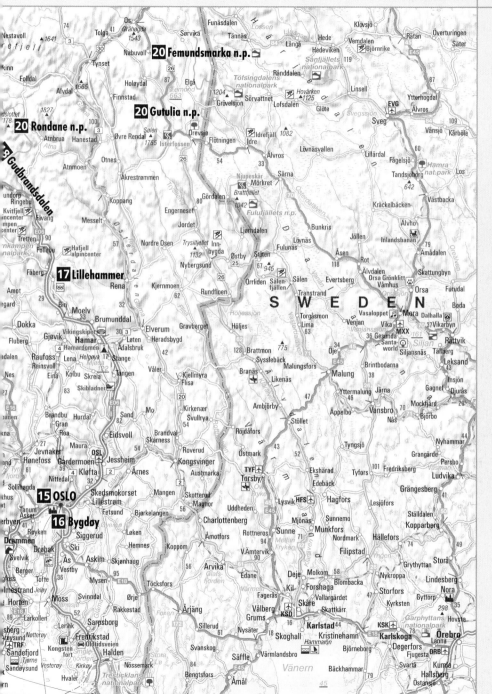

THE HIGHLIGHTS:
ØSTLANDET

INFO Open-air museum

Gausta points majestically toward the heavens (right). A historic stave church (inset below) stands adjacent to a modern white chapel and Torpo's community building. The mountainous area known as the Fillefjell connects Østlandet to the Sognefjord (below).

Hallingdal Museum, established in 1899, comprises 28 historic buildings and contains over 30,000 exhibits, which reflect the region's local culture in the most vivid fashion.

Rukkedalsvegen, 3540 Nesbyen;
Tel 32 07 14 85;
1 Jun–31 Aug Tues–Sun
11.00–16.00, or by request.

Gausta soars above the surrounding valleys. The highest mountain in Telemark (1,881 m/6,171 feet), it towers above other nearby peaks and offers spectacular views. From Gaustatoppen, the highest point, the view is panoramic, taking in the Skagerrak and the skerries, Tryvasshøgda and Oslo's tower, and the border with Sweden 175 km (109 miles) to the south. The Setesdalsheine mountain range and the Hardangervidda can also be seen, as well as the glacier Hardangerjøkulen and the summits of the Jotunheimen mountain range some 180 km (110 miles) further north. Hallingdal in Buskerud, a richly wooded area dotted with lakes, links the metropolis of Oslo with the mountains as it wends its way toward the western coast. Both sides of the valley are popular with walkers – the Norefjell in the south has been one of Norway's most popular ski resorts since hosting the Winter Olympic Games in 1952.

INFO Blues festival

A carved wooden frieze, depicting mythical creatures caught up in fighting, adorns the entrance area to the Heddal chapel (right). As is commonly the case in stave churches, this building was not constructed within a town but rather in an isolated location of unique natural beauty (below).

Every year at the beginning of August, Europe's most famous Blues festival explodes into life 120 km (75 miles) south-west of Oslo, in Notodden, attracting the greats of the international Blues world.

Tickets go on sale in May; Tel 81 53 31 33. www.bluesfest.no, www.billetservice.no

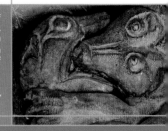

HEDDAL 🔢14

A village in Telemark near the "Blues town" of Notodden, Heddal, is home to the oldest remaining stave church in the world. Boasting a three-level roof and crowned by elegant turrets and towers, it is regarded as one of the most beautiful examples of its kind. Erected in the 13th century, it was rebuilt in the 1950s.

Alterations carried out during the Protestant Reformation have been dismantled, so that the church's appearance is now much the same as it would have been when the building was completed in 1242. Medieval worshippers would have laid down their weapons in the recess before the sanctuary, before

entering. According to legend, the master builder was a troll called Finne – who eventually fled the region because he could not stand the sound of the church bells. An exhibition in the Ministers Barn (also containing a cafe and shop) explains the history of the church and an open-air museum is nearby.

During the Middle Ages, the symbols of Christ, the Holy Family, and the Apostles were as prevalent in Norwegian art as elsewhere, but in the era following the Reformation more everyday themes began to emerge. The Lutheran clergyman and his family depicted here (right), and the infant Jesus (far right), can be found in Ringebu stave church. The other motifs shown below left hail from the churches in Eidsborg and Gol, while the images below middle and below right are from churches in Hedalen, Eidsborg again, and Lom.

Norway's wooden stave churches are the most important cultural monuments and heritage sites to have been built during the centuries-long era of Christianization. While the towns saw the construction of stone churches, such as the Trondheim and Stavanger cathedrals, around 1,000 stave churches were built in rural areas following the reign of King Olav the Holy (995–1030). The most interesting features of these one- or three-aisled wooden buildings are the characteristic pillars (staves) supporting the roof, set at right angles to each other, from where the churches get their name. The outer walls are made up of planks inserted into a frame. It is still unclear whether the use of staves in this way (often compared to ship's masts) actually stems from shipbuilding techniques or from the traditional architecture of the halls of the Nordic kings. Also characteristic of stave churches are the steeply sloping roofs with several tiers.

After the Reformation, the majority of the stave churches were torn down. A few were rebuilt elsewhere, simply for their aesthetic appeal, including the Vang church, which, in 1844, was rebuilt in the high mountains of Krummhübel in Silesia. Knut Hamsun (1859–1952), who won the Nobel Prize for Literature, was baptized in Garmo stave church, now the main focus of the Maihaugen open-air museum in Lillehammer. Very few stave churches remain intact in Norway today.

THE HIGHLIGHTS: ØSTLANDET

INFO The Bergen Line

In 1924, Norway's greatest sculptor Gustav Vigeland (1869–1943) created a whole sculptural landscape made up of several hundred individual sculptures in the Frogner Park (right: The Monolith). Below: Oslo's City Hall was built between 1931 and 1950 in a classic modern design.

The journey along the Bergen Line from Oslo to Bergen is an experience not to be missed, passing such sights as the Hardangervidda plateau and reaching a height of 1,222 m (4,009 feet). It is also worth taking a trip to Myrdal along the Flåm Line.
NSB Customer Services;
Tel 81 50 08 88. www.nsb.no

The university city of Oslo, is a busy capital and both Norway's largest port and its busiest transport hub, being also the focus of Norway's international communications and trade. Founded in 1050 by the Viking king Harald III Hardråde ("Harald the Ruthless") and set in a spectacular landscape of water, skerries, mountains, and woodland in the inner Oslofjord, its population now numbers around 530,000, with the whole whole metropolitan area containing 750,000 of Norway's 4.6 million residents. Jointly with Tokyo, it is the most expensive city in the world in terms of cost of living. The top of the 317-m (1,040-foot) high Holmenkollen, easily accessible by subway, is home to Scandinavia's most famous ski jump. From the top of the jump, a popular viewing point, the urban sprawl reaches out toward the Oslofjord with its cultural landmarks, residential districts, parks, and shopping malls. (See also pp. 163, 176.)

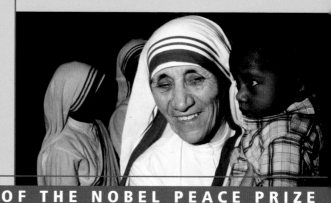

Albanian Catholic nun Mother Teresa (right) was awarded the Nobel Peace Prize by the king of Norway in 1979. Human rights activist Wangari Maathai (below) received the same award 25 years later, in 2004. Below right, bottom: The bust of the prize's founder, which stands in front of the Nobel Institute building.

The Swedish industrialist and inventor of dynamite Alfred Nobel (1833–1896) gave instructions in his will for the creation of a yearly "prize", funded by his bequest, to be granted to the individuals "who, during the preceding year, have conferred the greatest benefit on mankind". The first Nobel Prizes were accordingly awarded on 10 December 1901, the fifth anniversary of their founder's death, in Stockholm and Christiania (as Oslo was then known). Despite gaining independence from Sweden in 1905, Norway and Oslo did not lose their right to confer the most iconic of all the Nobel Prizes, the Nobel Peace Prize, traditionally awarded by the Norwegian monarch, while the Swedish king awards the prizes in the remaining categories in Stockholm. The Norwegian parliament is responsible for electing the five people, on renewable six-year terms, who make up the Nobel Peace Prize selection committee. The inspiration for a Peace Prize endowment came from the Austrian pacifist Bertha von Suttner, the author of *Lay Down Your Arms*, who was awarded the prize in 1905.

On the 100th anniversary of Norway's independence, King Harald V and King Carl XVI Gustaf of Sweden opened the Nobel Fredssenter (Nobel Peace Center) in Oslo, opposite the Oslo City Hall. Nobel Peace Prize laureates include Norwegian explorer Fridtjof Nansen, who originated the Nansen Passport, an internationally recognized ID card for stateless refugees.

THE HIGHLIGHTS: ØSTLANDET

The Gokstad, built by the Vikings (right), now kept in Oslo's Viking Ship Museum, was powered by 16 pairs of oarsmen. Below: The expedition undertaken by Thor Heyerdahl (1914–2002) in 1970 on *Ra II* (Kon-Tiki Museum, Oslo) was designed to establish whether contact would have been possible between Africa and Central America in ancient times.

TIP Museum restaurant

The Norwegian Museum of Cultural History's restaurant Arkadia & Torgkaféne offers tasty, traditional dishes.

Museumsveien 10, 0287 Oslo; Tel 22 12 37 00; 2 Jan–4 May 11.00–16.00, 15 May–14 Sept 11.00–18.00, 15 Sept–23 Dec 11.00–16.00.

Bygdøy, a residential area on a heavily wooded peninsula in the Oslofjord (west of the capital city), is home to the most important museum complex in the whole of Norway. The exhibits in the Vikingskipshuset (Viking Ship Museum) date from the Viking era and include ships such as the richly decorated Oseberg, which was used in sheltered waters on ceremonial occasions and measures 21.58 m (70.8 feet) in length and at least 5 m (16 feet) across. The Gokstad was an ocean-going vessel, discovered in 1880 in the Jongshaug burial mound near Sandefjord. The Fram Museum houses the legendary Arctic ship *Fram*, used by the explorer Roald Amundsen (1872–1928) who became the first man to reach the South Pole in 1911. Bygdoy is also home to the Norsk Sjøfartsmuseum (Norwegian Maritime Museum), the Norsk Folkemuseum (Norwegian Museum of Cultural History, an open-air museum), and the Kon-Tiki Museum containing Thor Heyerdahl's raft.

King Harald V (b. 1937) has been on the Norwegian throne since 1991 (below right). His son, Crown Prince Haakon (b. 1973), married commoner Mette-Marit in 2001 (right); three years later, Princess Ingrid Alexandra, Norway's first female heir to the throne was born. Oslo's castle is the royal residence (below).

THE NORWEGIAN MONARCHY: DEMOCRATICALLY ELECTED

The King's Council in Norway is the only democratically elected example of its kind in Europe. On 7 June 1905, the Storting (Parliament) of the Kingdom of Norway declared the dissolution of the union with Sweden, which had been in existence since 1814, and relieved the union's King Oscar II of Norway's rule, a decision supported by the majority of voters in a referendum. Not wanting to be crowned by politicians but rather by his own people, when the Danish Prince Carl (married to Maud, daughter of English King Edward VII), was offered the throne, the charismatic prince called for a further referendum. The resulting parliamentary debates showed opponents of the monarchy to be firmly in the minority, while the main supporting argument was that the Eidsvoll Constitution established in 1814 was approved by the nation, with historical precedent for a king. In November 1905, Carl was chosen with a majority of 259,563 to 622,641, and took the name Haakon VII. His coronation took place on 22 June 1906 in Nidaros Cathedral, Trondheim, a ceremony that emphasized the Christian values on which the new Norwegian democracy would be based. Haakon VII was the first Norwegian king for more than half a millennium. The last monarch to have ruled Norway alone, Haakon VI Magnusson, died in 1380. King Harald V is in line of succession to the British throne, though there are a good number of other royals in front of him.

INFO Olympic Park

Above: Small cabins are dotted about beside the cross-country and downhill ski runs in the upper part of Lillehammer. The pedestrianized part of Storgata (Lillehammer's main street) is a popular area for walking. Below: Everyday life from years gone by is recreated at Maihaugen Museum.

During the summer, Lillehammer's Olympic facilities can be used by the general public. Anyone brave enough can visit the bobsleigh and luge run, and career down the valley at 100 kph (60 mph) in a four-man bob.
Håkons Hall, 2601 Lillehammer; Tel 61 05 42 00; mid-Jun–mid-Aug 9.00–20.00 daily.

LILLEHAMMER AND MAIHAUGEN MUSEUM 🔢

The town of Lillehammer, closely associated with the Olympic Games, covers the area between Mjøsa, the largest lake in Norway, Gudbrandsdalen, the "valley of valleys", and the fjell region. The view from the Lysgårdsbakkene ski jump in the Olympic Park takes in the peaks and glaciers of the Rondane and Jotunheimen mountain ranges. Varying between wild fjells and cultivated land, the countryside here has been attracting its fair share of visitors and artists since the 19th century, and in particular to Lillehammer. Maihaugen, an area of undulating hills on the town's periphery, has been transformed into a park and is home to the largest open-air museum in northern Europe. During the summer months, visitors can see what everyday life was like in times gone by – people can be seen chopping wood, spinning yarn, preparing meals, and eating together in halls just as they did in the 19th century. (See also p. 163.)

THE HIGHLIGHTS: ØSTLANDET

INFO Peer Gynt Festival

Peer Gynt is supposed to have lived on the Håga Mound near Vinstra in Gudbrandsdalen (below). The Peer Gynt Vegen runs across the gently undulating fjell, with its abundant small lakes (inset below), which stretches between Gausdal and Gudbrandsdalen. Right: Walking in Skeikampen.

The ten-day-long culture festival inspired by Henrik Ibsen's play *Peer Gynt* begins every year at the end of July. A variety of outdoor shows take place at Galavatnet (lake) including performances of Grieg's orchestral suite *Peer Gynt*.
Vinstra Skysstasjon, 2640 Vinstra; Tel 61 29 47 70. www.peergynt.no

The "valley of valleys" – the name bestowed on this fertile valley by the Romantic poet Henrik Wergeland – stretches out to the national parks of Jotunheimen, Rondane, Dovre, and Dovrefjell-Sunndalsfjella. It is also the home of the legendary figure Peer Gynt, immortalized in literature by Norway's most important playwright Henrik Ibsen (1828–1906). The Gudbrandsdalslågen carves out a path through the Gudbrandsdalen, ending 203 km (126 miles) away in Mjøsa near Lillehammer, the largest lake in the country. For centuries, since Viking times, this river was Norway's most important communications and transport route between the east and central part of the country: in Dombås, all routes – including the historic King's and Pilgrim's routes (now hiking trails), and the European route E6 as well as the railway line leading from Oslo – head north away from Gudbrandsdalen, across the Dovrefjell to Trondheim.

INFO Besseggen Ridge

When September brings a seasonal glow to the lower altitudes, the Nautgardstinden still shines through in purest white (right). In February, the gently flowing Sjoa River beneath the Sjolikampen freezes over (inset below). Below: In "The Home of the Giants".

The most popular route along the Besseggen Ridge takes five to seven hours, and provides magnificent views the whole of its length from Memurubu to Gjendesheim. The well-maintained hiking route climbs to a height of 1,700 m (5,600 feet).
Tourist information:
Tel 61 21 29 90.

At 2,469 m (8,100 feet), Galdhøpiggen is the highest peak in Scandinavia. The ice-covered mountain range here (jagged and craggy on the Vestlandet side) includes another 200 or so peaks that also exceed 2,000 m (6,500 feet). The Østland side, on the other hand, presents an altogether more gentle perspective. It was the poet Aasmund Olavsson Vinje, who, in the 19th century, named this whole mountainous area "The Home of the Giants" (Jotunheimen), a name already well known from old Norse literature. Situated in the middle of these high mountains, the Jotunheimen National Park was created in 1980 and covers an area of 1,151 sq. km (444 sq. miles). It is Norway's most accessible region for walking and mountain climbing. At the eastern edge of the park is what is probably the most famous hiking route in the whole of Norway: the Besseggen mountain ridge, which runs alongside the emerald-green Lake Gjende.

THE HIGHLIGHTS: ØSTLANDET

Nature's life cycle unfolds on Rondane's highest peaks (insets below, from left): snowfields in early summer; fiery hues in the fall; luxurious cottongrass in midsummer. Below: Gutulia National Park is home to bears, foxes, and elks. Right: The idyllic landscape in Femundsmarka National Park.

INFO Tours on horseback

Rondane National Park offers horseback tours of varying length and difficulty, led by experienced guides familiar with the area.

Rondane tourist information: Tel 61 23 66 50. Details of horseback tour providers can be found at www.visitrondane.com

Rondane is Norway's oldest national park. Its valleys, ravines, and peaks – the highest of which is Rondslottet at 2,178 m (7,146 feet) – as well as its boulder-strewn plains, morainic terraces, dead-ice crevasses, ridges and glacier cirques, marshes, fertile oases, and pinewood forests, all combine to create a spectac- ular region for hiking enthusiasts. Visitors can also stay on site if they wish, in a hotel located next to Rondvatnet (lake). In 2003, the Rondane's area was increased to 963 sq. km (372 sq. miles). Situated a few miles to the east, the Femundsmarka National Park with its many lakes is a haven for canoeists, anglers, and hikers. People also collect berries here in season. In 2003 its area was increased to 573 sq. km (221 sq. miles). Gutulia National Park, to the south of Femundsmarka, spans 23 sq. km (9 sq. miles) and mostly contains pinewood and spruce forests, as well as marshy wetlands on the Swedish border.

THE HIGHLIGHTS

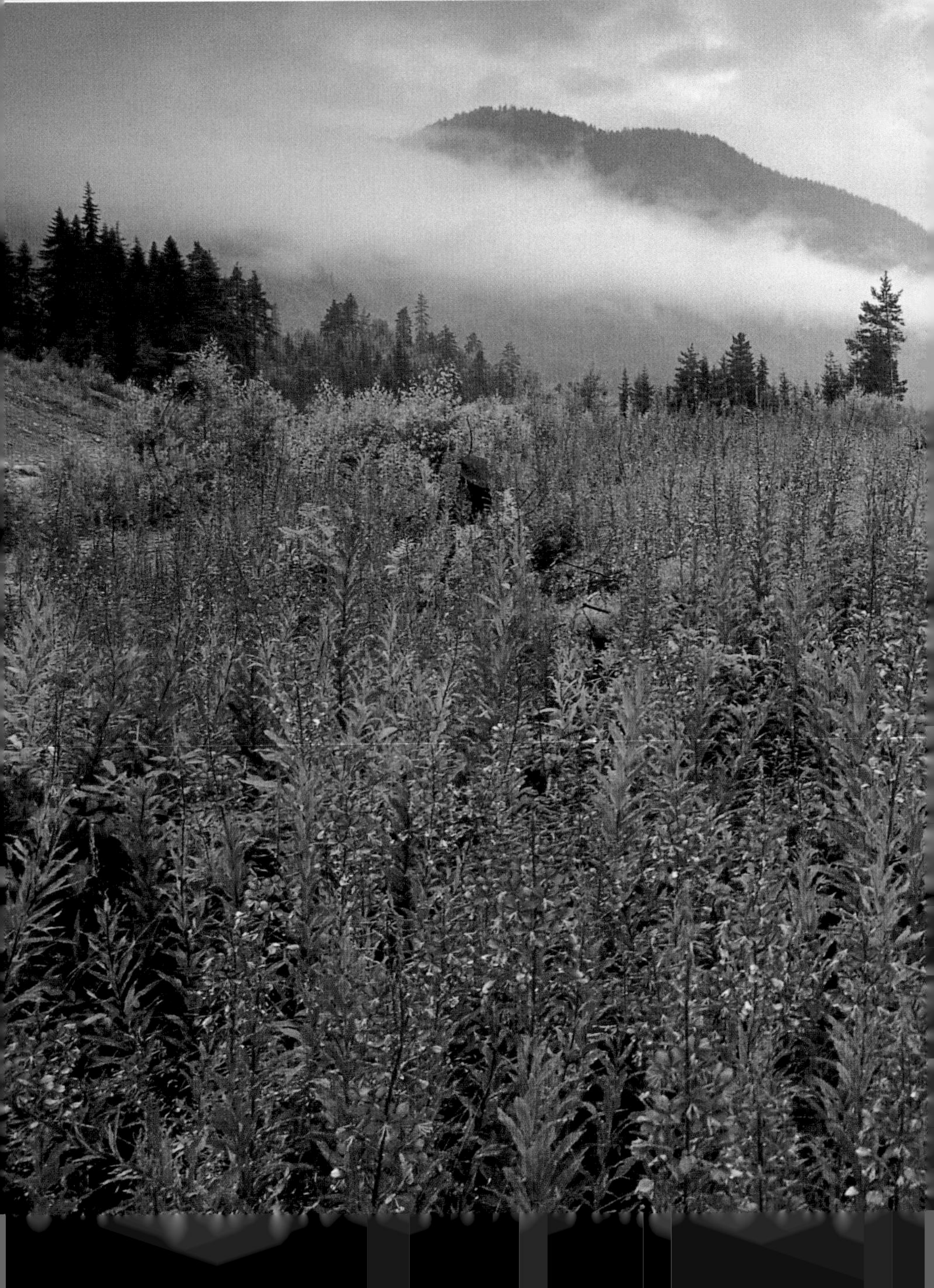

SØRLANDET

The region known as Sørlandet in southern Norway stretches from the skerries, the small rocky islands on the fringe of Skagerrak, to the fjells either side of the Otra River, which flows through the historic and picturesque Setesdal valley. The largest city in Sørlandet, and the seat of the Vest-Agder province government, is Kristiansand, well known for its ports and almost equally renowned as the home of Mette-Marit, Crown Prince Haakon's popular wife. Sørlandet's other urban areas such as Aust-Agder's provincial capital Arendal, are spread out across seven islands. Known as the "Venice of Scandinavia", in the 18th and 19th centuries Arendal's wealth was based on shipping.

21 Lindesnes

22 Skerry island fringe

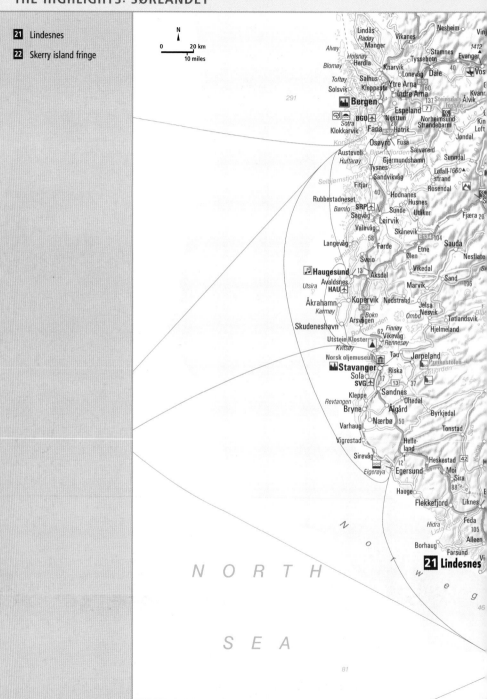

N

0   20 km

10 miles

Nesheim
Lindås   Vikanes   Vinj
Radøy   Manger
Alvøy   Stamnes   1412
Holsnøy   Tyssebotn   Evanger
Blomøy   Herdla   Kharvik   40   Vos
Lonevåg   Dale
Toftøy   Salhus   Ytre Arna   60
Solsvik   Kleppestø   Indre Arna   Kvanr.
Bergen   137 Steinsdals Alvik
fossen
Espeland   7
BGO   Nesttun   Norheimsund   Kin
Sotra   28   Strandebarm   Loft
Klokkarvik   Fana   Hatrik   Jondal
Korsfjorden   Osøyrø   Fusa
Austevoll   Bjørnafjorden   Sævareid
Huttarøy   Gjermundshamn   Sunndal
Tysnes   Løfall-1660
Sandvikvåg   strand
Selbjørnsfjorden   Fitjar   Rosendal
40   Hodnanes
Rubbestadneset   Husnes
Bømlo   SRP   Sunde   Utåker   Fjæra 26
Søgvåg
Valevåg   Leirvik
Skånevik
Langevåg   58   E134 104
Bømlafjorden   Førde   Etne   Sauda
Sveio   Ølen   Nesflate
Haugesund   13   Vikedal   S.
Utsira   Avaldsnes   Aksdal   Sand   196
HAU   Marvik
Åkrahamn   Kopervik   Nedstrand   Jelsa
Karmøy   E39   Nesvik
Bokn   Ombo   Tøtlandsvik
Skudeneshavn   Arsvågen
Boknafjorden   Finnøy   62   Hjelmeland
Utstein Kloster   Vikevåg
Kvitsøy   Rennesøy
Norsk oljemuseum   Tau   Jørpeland
Stavanger   Riska   Preikestolen
Sola   Lysefjorden
SVG   17   13   37
Kleppe   Sandnes
Revtangen   Oltedal
Bryne   Ålgård
Nærbø   50   Byrkjedal
Varhaug   Tonstad
Vigrestad   Helle-
land
Sirevåg   Heskestad   42
12   Moi
Eigerøya   Egersund   Sira
88
Hauge
Flekkefjord   Liknes
Hidra   Feda
Listahalv.   105
Borhaug   Alleen
Farsund
21 Lindesnes

N O R T H

S E A

Fagernes Leira Åmot
Hemsedal Aurdal Flatøydegard 29 32 62
Skicenter E16 Bagn Dokka Biri Moelv
Flåmsbana Torpo Gol Reinli Fluberg Gjøvik Brumunddal Elverum Gravberget
al Finse Hol Stavkirke Vikingskipet 30 3 Heradsbygd
Geilo Nesbyen Hedalen Begnadalen Raufoss Lena Helgøya Stange 42 Våler Kjellmyra
Haugastøl 100 Dagali Gulsvik Nes Eina Kolbu Skreia Tangen Flisa
ssli 7 Skibladner 83 20
Dyranut danger-
ngervidda Skrekken Uvdal Rødberg Gråfjell Brandbu Hurdal Sand Mo Kirkenær
▲1429 134 1466 Gran Røa Svullrya
onalpark Uvdal Eggedal Sokna Eidsvoll Brandval 54
vidda stavkirke Noresund 27 Maura Skarnes Roverud
Bakko 161 Krøderen Jevnaker OSL 54 Kongsvinger
O R W A Y Prestfoss Tyristrand Hønefoss Gardermoen Jessheim Austmarka
Vikersund Nittedal 59 Kløfta 2 Ärnes 2
Rjukan Geithus Sollihøgda Skedsmokorset Sørumsand Mangen Skotterud
er 1630 Vemork Flesberg Åmot OSLO Slattum 32 Fetsund Bjørkelangen Magnor
Gaustatoppen Tanum Lille- Charlottenberg 56
Rauland Bossbøen 1882 Lampeland Hokksund Lierbyen Asker strøm Amotfors
Gransherad Saggrenda Mjøndalen Drammen Nesodden Siggerud Løken Koppom
Sauland Heddal Kongsberg Røyken Hemnes Arvika 56
Amot stavkirke Skollenborg Svelvik Drøbak Ski Askim Skjønhaug
Dalen Seljord Heddal Notodden Hof Berger Tofte Vestby Mysen 95 Töcksfors
1521 Kvitseid Bø Hvittingfoss Holmestrand Jeløy Svinndal Ørje E18
Vrådal Gvarv Nordagutu Svarstad 85 Horten Moss Rakkestad Årjäng
Lunde Ulefoss Siljan Andebu 89 Larkollen 52 Sarpsborg Sillerud
Fyresdal Nissedal Vrangfoss Skien Tønsberg Netterøy Fredrik- Sarpsborg 61
sluser Porsgrunn Kvelde Åsgårdstrand stad Oldtidsveien Svanskog
Tveitsund Drangedal Stathelle Sandefjord Tjøme Kongsten Halden
Neslandsvatn Langesund Larvik Sandøysund Vesterøy fort Kirkøy Nössemark 84
Gjerstad Nevlunghavn Stavern Hvaler Bengtsfors
Amli Kil Kragerø Strömstad Skee Billingsfors Dals 81
Dølemo Søndeled Levang Koster- Ed Länged
Byglandsfjord Vegårshei Risør Lyngør öarna Töftedal Håverud
Evje Nelaug Tvedestrand Grebbestad SWEDEN Smeberg Bäckefors Bränna
Vegusdal Svenes Hällristningar Tanumshede Högsäter Mellerud
Herefoss Blakstad Eydehavn Fjällbacka Färgelanda
Iveland Rykene Tromøya Dingle Stigen Brålanda
Birkeland Fevik Arendal Hunnebostrand Munkedal Troll Såtenäs
Vennesla Grimstad Nordens Ark Brastad Fagerhult hätte Vänersborg
KRS Lillesand Kungshamn Uddevalla kanal Vargön
Kristiansand Håvåg Skerry island fringe Lysekil Herrestad Trollhättan THN
Christiansholm 22 Fiskebäckskil Henån Orust Ljungskile Sjuntorp Grästorp
Flekkerøy Ellös Varekil Nossebro
Stenungsund Lilla Edet
Skagerrak Skärhamn Lödöse Sollebrunn
Tjörn Älvängen Alingsås
Kode Kungälv Nödinge-Nol Lerum
Marstrand Hisingen Lerum
Skagens museum Grenen Hönö Partille
Skagen Göteborg Landvetter Bollebygd
Hirtshals Tannis Bugt Albæk Liseberg GOT
DENMARK Albæk Bugt Strandby Billdal Källered Lindome

THE HIGHLIGHTS: SØRLANDET

INFO Lighthouse

A series of sparse rocks make up Norway's southern headland (right) on the jagged coast of Lindesnes (below). Norway's first lighthouse recently celebrated its 350th anniversary: in 1655, 30 candles were used to light the tower originally on this spot. The current "Lindesnesfyr" (below right) dates from 1915.

The lighthouse at Lindesnes represents centuries of tradition. An exhibition inside the tower explains the history of the lighthouse.

4520 Lindesnes; Tel 97 54 08 15; 1 May–30 Jun and 14 Aug–8 Oct 11.00–17.00 daily, 1 Jul–13 Aug 9.00–21.00 daily, rest of year Sat, Sun 11.00–17.00.

Lindesnes is the most southerly point on the Norwegian mainland, which at a latitude of 57° 58´ N is on a level with the Hebridean Islands off the north Scottish coast, and with Hudson Bay in Canada. Being the "southern headland", Lindesnes ranks as one of Sørland's most popular attractions, even if most tourists are only interested in seeing the lighthouse and its museum. Visitors wanting to continue from here as far as the actual southernmost point of the Norwegian mainland, found on the rocky hilltops stretching into the sea a little further away, will find themselves mostly alone and undisturbed (even in high season) during the hour-long walk there and back. Looking out from the southernmost point, where the rocks plunge steeply down toward the sea, the view is one of a vast emptiness – the ocean, punctuated by a scattering of islands, seems to stretch to infinity. (See also p. 164.)

INFO Town museum

The port of Lillesand (right) on the Sørland coast is a popular destination thanks to its historic wooden architecture. The famous Blindleia shipping route begins in Lillesand and runs through the skerries, many of which are densely wooded and are popular locations for getaway homes (below).

One of the most historic buildings in Lillesand, dating from 1827, houses a private collection of everyday household objects and furniture, illustrating what life would have been like here many years ago.

Carl Knudsengården, 4790 Lillesand; Tel 37 26 16 92; open by arrangement.

The coast of Sørland is a sun-kissed paradise for bathers, anglers, and lovers of water sports, protected from the open sea by a string of skerries (small rocky islands). Almost all the ports run boat tours in the form of mini-cruises around the skerries. The Blindleia, a waterway as narrow as 10 m (33 feet) across in places, which runs between Lillesand and Høvåg, near Kristiansand, is regarded as the most scenic route for boat trips throughout the Sørland coastal area. Unlike the isles between Kristiansand and Lillesand, the 200 or so islands and islets of the skerry fringe between Kristiansand and Mandal are largely undeveloped, with many of them serving as important habitats and breeding areas for seabirds. Mandal, the most southerly town in Norway, boasts the longest sandy beach in the country, protected by the string of skerries: 800-m (2,600-feet) long Sjøsanden is a very popular destination in summer. (See also pp. 164, 165.)

Right, from left: A poster from the 1920s advertising the psychological drama of *The Lady from the Sea*; Emily Stevens playing the title role of the tragic wife *Hedda Gabler*; child actors in *A Doll's House*. A portrait of Henrik Ibsen from 1896 (inset below right), and the Ibsen Museum in Oslo, where Norway's most important poet and playwright died (below).

IBSEN: "BE YOURSELF"

Henrik Ibsen (1828–1906) was born in Skien, the capital of Telemark. From 1844 to 1850 he was an apprentice pharmacist in Grimstad, where there are now a number of museums dedicated to him: the Reimanngården on Vestregate 3 is a reconstruction of the pharmacy where he served his apprenticeship. Ibsenhuset contains the poet's first independent lodgings, where he wrote his debut play *Catilina*. In 2006, the Ibsen Museum in Oslo reopened the 'playwright's final home, where Ibsen lived from 1895 until his death 11 years later, completely restoring and furnishing it as it would have been in Ibsen's time.

Ibsen's plays cast a very critical eye over the society and mores of the time, and pioneered naturalism on the stage. *Peer Gynt*, a play in verse, was the 39-year-old's first worldwide success: the concept of "be yourself" is used as a theme running through the entire work. Romantic composer Edvard Grieg's incidental music for the play, as well as his two "Peer Gynt" suites, which represent the content of the play in musical form, had no small influence on the success of the work. Ibsen's 1877 play *Pillars of Society* created the genre of the critical comedy of manners, denouncing the double standards of the middle class. In *A Doll's House*, written in 1879, the character of Nora, wife of banker Torvald, became a role model for women fighting for female emancipation.

Wooden houses painted a brilliant white (right) cluster around the port of Flekkefjord, on the western border of Sørland. Wood imported from the Netherlands was shipped into the port and used for building houses and dykes. It was shortly after the devastating fires of 1861 that Risør (below) was reinvented as the "white town".

RISØR AND THE WHITE TOWNS: PEARLS OF THE SØRLAND RIVIERA

The luminous white towns along the sea's edge are the architectural gems of the Sørland coastline, the "whitest" being Risør, located at the end of a peninsula in the Skagerrak. Wandering around Risør's 500 or so wooden houses, many painted white and some the traditional Falu red, is like stepping back in time in a living museum. They have been named an "area of particular historical interest" and are therefore afforded special protection. The "white town" was built in 1861 following a huge fire that had left few buildings standing other than the baroque church (completed in 1647). Over the following years, enormous numbers of these white-painted houses were built, in a mix of Empire and Biedermeier styles. Stately homes in the "Swiss style" – that is, tall with multiple floors and overhanging roof ridges – lent an air of magnificence and gaiety to the surroundings. Risør's wealth is thanks to its port, which stays mostly ice-free (even in winter) and serves as a base for the export of ice blocks to the London fish markets. To complete the scene, even Risør's chalk rocks are dressed in "white", the most famous being the 45-m (148-foot) high Risørflekken. Once used as a navigational aid for sailors, it is now popular for its supreme panorama across the entire Sørland coastline – the view from the top across to the open sea is magnificent. The picturesque Risør attracts many artists and today derives most of its income from tourism.

Right: Simek AS in Flekkefjord is one of Norway's largest shipyards, supplying fishing boats, ferries, and other vessels built using components produced by high-technology companies throughout the country. Below and below left: Ship propellers at the Rolls-Royce Marine AS plant in Flekkefjord.

FROM FARMING COUNTRY TO LAND OF TECHNOLOGY

In the space of just 100 years, Norway has developed from being a country based on a rural economy into an ultra-modern and technologically advanced state producing goods of world class, with an excellent education system and financial stability. This change was already underway by 1905 when the union between Sweden and Norway was dissolved, and Norwegian independence was declared. Also in the same year, Sam Eyde founded Norsk Hydro in Notodden, now the largest of Norway's industrial corporate groups. Building on an invention by the physicist Kristian Birkeland, Norsk Hydro grew into a fertilizer manufacturer that spearheaded worldwide production. Light metals (in particular aluminum products), along with energy (wind and hydroelectricity), are now this corporate group's main business concerns, with activities in around 40 countries. A total of 40 percent of all Norway's goods and services are exported, with imports making up only just over a third of the gross national product. The country's most important products are oil, gas, and minerals, as well as fish and seafood. Norway's economy was given a further boost by the oil boom that began in 1971, and by the digital revolution. Norway is now a leader in research and education, encouraging businesses to develop cost-effective and environmentally friendly ways forward in software and communications technology, the aerospace industry, engineering and bioengineering.

THE HIGHLIGHTS

TRØNDELAG

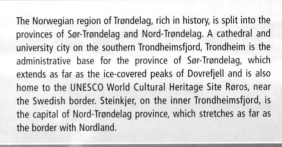

The Norwegian region of Trøndelag, rich in history, is split into the provinces of Sør-Trøndelag and Nord-Trøndelag. A cathedral and university city on the southern Trondheimsfjord, Trondheim is the administrative base for the province of Sør-Trøndelag, which extends as far as the ice-covered peaks of Dovrefjell and is also home to the UNESCO World Cultural Heritage Site Røros, near the Swedish border. Steinkjer, on the inner Trondheimsfjord, is the capital of Nord-Trøndelag province, which stretches as far as the border with Nordland.

N

0   20 km

10 miles

N O R W E G I A N

96

Halten E

S E A

Helle

Frøya

Titran   Hamn

Frøyfjorden   Fi

Hopen   Hitra

Dyrnes   Forsnes

Smøla

Korsvoll

Vinsternes   Kyrks

Leira

KSU Tustna   Ertvågøy

Kristiansund   Tømmervåg   Vi

Reinsvik

70 Frei   79 Enge

Halsa

Averøya

Bud   Eide

Elnesvågen   Nordmøre   Tingvoll   Skei

Steinshamn   E39   68   Seljebø

Gossen   Hjelset

Molde MOL 63 Kleive

Austnes   Otrøy   Eidsvåg

AES   Midsund Moldefjorden Sølsnes

Vigra   Brattvåg   Tomrefjord   Vestnes   Åfarnes   Sunndalsøra

Godøy Ålesund   Vatne   E39   Isfjorden   69 Gjøra

Atlanterhavsparken   Spjelkavik E136   Sunndal

Runde   Langevåg 59   Sjøholt Trestjord 60 Åndalsnes

Hareid   Sykkylven   Trolltindan Mardalen 1871

Fosnavåg Ulsteinvik   Stordalen

Sandsøy   Stranda   Trollstigen 1797   **25** Dovrefjell-Sunndalsfjell

Vartdal   Linge   Øverdalen

Leikanger   Arvik Ørsta Sunnmøre   Eidsdalen   Stuguflåten Sn

Kopárnes Volda Sæbø Leknes   Puttega 105   2286

HOV   Kvitegga   1999 E136   Erka D

Selje   Folkestad 1691   Susystre Geiranger

Aheim   Hellesylt   Geirangerfjorden

52 Stårheim   Grotli 73   Skarsstind   Dombås

Isane Nordfjordeid 44   Stryn 50 Videsæter   1883   D

Svelgen   Bismo   46

Staume SDN Sandane Olden   Lom Vågåmo No

Norddal 1385   59   Jostedalsbreen nasjonalpark   Sotasæter Norsk Fjell 15 62

Byrkjelo Briksdal   museum

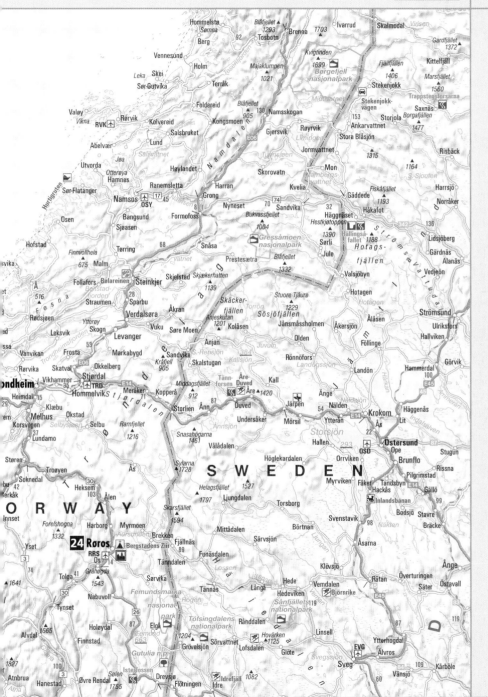

Hommelstø
Sømna
Berg
Blåfjellet ▲ 1293
Tosbotn
Brenna 1703
Ivarrud
Skalmodal
Gardfjället 1372

Vennesund
Holm
Kvigtinden 1699
Børgefjell nasjonalpark
Fjällfjällen
Kittelfjäll
Majaklumpen 1021

Leka Skei
Sør-Gutvika
Terråk
Stekenjokk
Marsfjället 1560
Stekenjokk-vägen
Trappstegsforsarna

Valøy Vikna RVK
Rørvik
Kølvereid
Foldereid
Blåfjellet 130
Namsskogan 905
Kongsmoen
Saxnäs
Borgafjällen 1477
Storjola
153
Ankarvattnet

Abelvær
Lund
Salsbruket
Gjersvik
Røyrvik
Lillingen
Stora Blåsjön
Risbäck

Jøa
Utvorda
Otterøya
Hamnes
Høylandet
Jormvattnet
Mon
1315
1164
S-Sjouten

Sør-Flatanger
Ranemsletta
Harran
Skorovatn
Kvelia
Gäddede
Fiskåfjället 1193
Harrsjö

Namsos OSY
17 45
Grong
74
Sandvika
32
Håkafot
Norråker

Osen
Bangsund
Sjøåsen
Formofoss
Nyneset
Bukvassfjellet 1004
Häggnäset
Hestkjøtoppen
136

Hofstad
Finnvollhøa
675 Malm
Tørring 68
Snåsa
Gressåmoen nasjonalpark
1390
Sørli
Jule
Hallingsåfallet 1188
Hotags-fjällen
Lidsjöberg
Gärdnäs
Alanås

svika
Å
Follafors Bølareinen
Steinkjer
Prestesætra
Blåfjellet 1332
Valsjöbyn
Vedjeön

516
Straumen
Sparbu
Skjelstad Skjækerhatten 1139
Stuore Tjåure
Hotagen
Strömsund

Rødsjøen
Ytterøy Skogn
Verdalsøra
Åkran
Anjeskutan 1201
Skäcker-fjällen Torrön
Sösjöfjällen
1229
Ålåsen
Ulriksfors

Leksvik
Levanger
Vuku
Søre Moen
Kolåsen
Jänsmåssholmen
Åkersjön
Hallviken

Vanvikan
Frosta 53
Markabygd
Sandvika Kråfjell 905
Anjan
Rönnofors
Olden
Föllinge
Görvik

Rørvika
Skatval
Okkelberg
Skalstugan
Landön
Hammerdal 100

ndheim Vikhammer Stjørdal
Hommelvik
Meråker
Middagsfjället
Tänn-forsen
Åre-Duved
Kall
Ånge
E45

Heimdal 15
Klæbu
Kopperå 87
Storlien Ånn
Åre 1420
Järpen 54
Nälden
Häggenås

Melhus Okstad
Korsvegen Selbu
Ramfjellet 1216
Duved
Undersåker
Mörsil
Ytterån
Krokom
Lit
Ås

Lundamo
Snasahögarna 1461
Vålådalen
Hallen 293
Östersund OSD Öpe
Stugun

Støren
Troøyen Ås
Sylarna 1728
SWEDEN
Höglekardalen
Orrviken
Brunflo
Rissna

Soknedal
Heksem 103
Ålen
Helagsfjället 1527
1797
Ljungdalen
Torsborg
Myrviken
Fåker
Tandsbyn
Hackås
Pilgrimstad
Gällö

ORWAY
Innset
Forelshogna 1332
Harborg
Myrmoen
Brekken
Skarsfjället 1594
Mittådalen
Särvsjön
Börtnan
Svenstavik
Åsarna
Bodsjö Stavre
Bräcke

Yset
24 Røros RRS Os
Bergstadens Ziir
Fjällnäs 89
Tänndalen
Funäsdalen
Klövsjö
Ånge

Tolga 41
Gråhøgda 1543
Sørvika
Tännäs
Långå
Hede
Hedeviken
Vemdalen
Björnrike
Rätan
Överturingen
Säter
Östavall

Nabuvoll
Femundsmarka nasjonalpark
Sånfjället 119 nationalpark
87
119

Tynset
Holøydal
Elgå
Töfsingdalens nationalpark
Rånddalen
Hovärken 1125
Linsell
Ytterhogdal

Alvdal 1665
Finnstad
1204
Grövelsjön
Sørvattnet
Lofsdalen
Glöte
EVG
Älvros

1827
Atnbrua
Hanestad
Øvre Rendal
Sølen 1755
Drevsjø
Flötningen Idre
Idrefjäll 1082
Sveg
Vänsjö
Kårböle

Ecological roulette: salmon farms were primarily created to conserve the overfished stocks of wild salmon (below: Atlantic salmon), but have had the opposite effect: cages packed to bursting point with farmed fish became infested with salmon lice, which killed much of the wild salmon population here. Below right: It is the pigment in the feed that gives salmon its pink hue, seen here being smoked.

OCEAN RESOURCES: FISHING AND AQUACULTURE

Although fishing makes up a mere 0.5 percent of the gross national product and the number of professional fishermen has halved to under 13,000 over the last 15 years, Norway is still one of the world's leading fishing nations – and in the light of its history, is likely to remain so for some time to come. Fishing permeates its culture and traditions, and is the reason why Norway does not respond to appeals from "green" organizations and other nations – the practices of whaling and seal hunting will continue, even if the rewards are only marginal. Cod, along with capelin and herring, are important for the economy, as is aquaculture, including salmon farming, an area in which Norway is a world leader. The most famous salmon-rich waters and traditionally the best fishing grounds are found in the north, and for more than a millennium, cod has been the main focus for Lofoten fishermen. Finnmark is the most important region for wild salmon – around 170 tons of salmon are caught there every year, 36 percent of Norway's entire salmon production. Namsos, Alta, and Sør-Varanger are legendary salmon fishing grounds, with an international reputation. As the quantities of salmon caught in the wild have halved since the 1980s, fishing companies have focused more and more on aquaculture, with artificial breeding grounds providing a freshly caught supply of this very popular fish all year round.

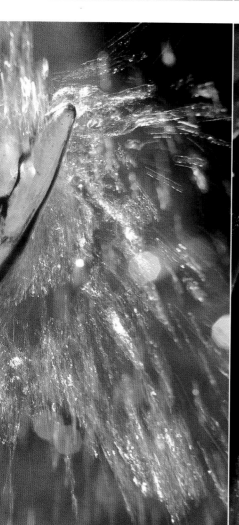

The facades of the warehouses standing on pillars along the waterfront form a photogenic backdrop (below): wooden buildings remain as witnesses to Trondheim's merchant tradition, including the rococo Stiftsgården palace (right). The Gamle Bybro (inset below), also known as the "Gate of Fortune", crosses over the Nidelva River in the nearby old town.

TIP Palmehaven

The Palmehaven in the Britannia Hotel has been Trondheim's principal restaurant since 1918. It serves classic Norwegian cuisine; evening diners can choose from an à la carte menu.

Dronningensgate 5, 7401 Trondheim; Tel 73 80 08 00; Tues–Sat 11.00–15.00 and from 18.00, Mon open for lunch only.

The city of Trondheim was built during the 17th century in sight of the Kristiansten fortress, and was originally christened Nidaros, a reference to its location (*os*) at the mouth of the Nid (now Nidelva) River. With 156,000 inhabitants, Trondheim is the third largest city in Norway after Oslo and Bergen. From the 18th century onward, this Norwegian city (important in the Middle Ages as the site for the coronation of kings and bishops) underwent a new lease of life as a base for scholarship and education. By 1760 the Norwegian Society of Sciences and Letters had been founded here. More recently, in 1910, Norway's first Institute of Technology opened its doors, and in 1968 the university began its first lectures – today, around 20 percent of Trondheim's inhabitants are students. This vibrant "old and young metropolis" offers a huge variety of cultural pursuits – from open-air events in the summer to the famous cathedral concerts. (See also pp. 166, 182.)

The oldest parts of the cathedral, containing spookily demonic-looking gargoyles (inset below), are the transept dating from 1152 and the chapter house built over the Olav Spring. The long Gothic chancel with three naves was next to be erected in 1186, followed by the western wall (right) with its rose window (below). The building work was completed in 1248.

Nidaros Cathedral in Trondheim is the largest example of a Gothic cathedral in Scandinavia, and the place where Norway's coronations take place. Spiritually significant during the Middle Ages as the most important pilgrimage site in northern Europe, the cathedral is once more gaining recognition: the old pilgrimage route from Oslo, which is associated with Santiago de Compostela and which passes over the Dovrefjell to the grave of Olav the Holy in Nidaros Cathedral and then on to Stiklestad, was reopened in 1997, having been relaid and signposted. A thousand years earlier in 997, the Christian Viking king Olav I Tryggvason established a royal court at the mouth of the Nidelva River, which was the precursor to the city of Nidaros (Trondheim's former name). By 1016, under Olav II the Holy, Nidaros had become the country's most important residence. King Olav II, killed during the Battle of Stiklestad against the pagan Germanic Norwegians and the occupying Danish forces, became the patron saint of Norway, a figurehead for a united Christian Norway free from foreign influence. Nidaros Cathedral was built over his grave and became a pilgrimage site. After the Reformation, however, Nidaros' significance diminished: it lost its archbishop, and the cathedral fell into disrepair. It was only reconstructed and restored in modern times, when Nidaros finally took the Danish name of "Dronthjem" – which became Trondheim.

THE HIGHLIGHTS: TRØNDELAG

INFO Mine tours

The octagonal church, built in 1784, is the only stone building in the historic mining town of Røros, and the town's landmark (below and insets below, top and middle). The miners lived in simple huts (inset below, bottom). Olavsgruva (Olav's Mine) is now a mining museum and educational center (right).

Visitors can directly experience mining life, 50 m (160 feet) underground, with the help of audiovisual effects. The tour visits the old Nyberget Mine (1650) and Olav's Mine, opened in 1936.

Rørosmuseet, 7374 Røros; Tel. 72 40 61 70; 20 Jun–15 Aug 10.30, 12.00, 14.00, 15,30, and 17.00 daily.

RØROS 24

Røros, with its 5,400 inhabitants, lies on the Swedish border, 630 m (2,067 feet) above sea level, and holds the record for the coldest temperature ever recorded in Norway at −50.4 °C (−58.7 °F) . It was in this cold pocket of land that in 1644 copper reserves were discovered, and the country's first copper smelter was estab- lished here. A shortage of qualified work- ers meant that miners had to be brought in from all over Europe, in particular from Germany. New metallic deposits were dis- covered and subsequently exhausted in rapid succession, allowing the town to expand continuously for some time. Røros is the best preserved historic mining town in Norway, and has been a protected UNESCO World Cultural Heritage Site since 1980. Copper was extracted here for more than 300 years (until 1977), the only interruption being when the works were damaged by a fire in the latter half of the 17th century – a deadly but com- mon problem in mining. (See also p. 166.)

THE HIGHLIGHTS: TRØNDELAG

INFO Musk ox safaris

The Dovrefjell-Sunndalsfjella National Park combines broad plateaus (below) and ice-covered high mountains. The sheer walls of the rocky plateau plunge down toward the several tributary valleys of the Sunndalsfjord in a series of 100-m (330-foot) high, steep rock faces (inset below).

The Dovrefjell National Park is one of the few places in the world where the powerful musk ox can still be seen running wild. From June to September, guided hikes offer visitors the chance to see these ice-age survivors.
Oppdal Booking; Tel 72 40 08 00.
www.moskussafari.no

"United and true until Dovre falls" – this was the oath sworn in Eisvoll in 1814 by the founding fathers as they approved the Constitution of the Democratic Kingdom of Norway, a constitution which stands to this day. At that time, the 2,286-m (7,500-foot) high Snøhetta (the highest peak in the Dovrefjell mountain range) was presumed to be the highest in all Norway. However, once the country had been fully surveyed, it became clear that Galdhøpiggen (2,469 m/8,100 feet) in the Jotunheimen mountain range overshadowed the "Snow Cap" unequivocally. In 1974, the highest parts of the Dovrefjell were given protected national park status because of their natural beauty, their rich variety of vegetation, which includes many rare plants, and the animals that live here. In 2002, the national park was extended to 1,693 sq. km (654 sq. miles) and renamed "Dovrefjell-Sunndalsfjella". Wild reindeer are indigenous to the park.

A menagerie of Norwegian wildlife (right, from left): oystercatcher; Black-legged Kittiwakes; puffin. Below left, from top: Lapwing; nesting Red-throated Loon; Arctic Terns feeding in mid-flight; sea eagle hunting fish. Below right, from top: Elk; reindeer; lynx; red fox. Below middle: Musk ox.

ANIMAL LIFE: FROM THE FOREST TO THE ARCTIC

The great variety of scenery that exists stretching across 12 latitude lines has spawned an equally varied selection of animals: the south of Norway is very similar to central Europe, whereas the high mountain plains and the north have an Arctic climate. The musk ox is the most recognizable symbol of the Arctic, and was introduced to the tundra landscape of Dovrefjell from Greenland. Humans and wolves are equally wary of musk oxen: both know that this seemingly ponderous herd animal will charge at lightning speed if in danger, and can gore or impale any creature seen as a threat. Lynxes, bears, and wolves are all still found in Norway's mountainous areas, even though their habitat is being commandeered almost exclusively to form national parks. Most of these animals avoid humans; however, if they feel threatened, bears can become particularly dangerous. The areas containing the largest populations of wild reindeer are Hardangervidda, Dovrefjell, and Rondane. The reindeer are hunted and a record is kept of the number officially killed – in 2005, for example, 860 wild reindeer were killed in Hardangervidda, 570 in the Snøhetta region, and 980 in the Rondane area. The reindeer population can only be estimated, however. Elks have been helped by the extensive logging outside the national parks: the areas of reforestation have provided a rich food supply, enabling their numbers to increase considerably over the last few decades.

NORDLAND

The magnificent north: the Nordland coastline, carved into a geographic jigsaw of deep fjords, along with its offshore islands, undoubtedly ranks among the most spectacular landscapes on Earth. The area is famous for its stunning scenery and wildlife safaris. From the Helgeland coastline in the south, containing the UNESCO World Heritage Site of the Vega Archipelago, it stretches north toward the Lofoten Islands, whose bizarrely shaped rock faces can tower up to 1,000 m (3,280 feet) above the surf crashing below. The Arctic Circle province of Nordland has 17,934 km (11,144 miles) of coastline – by far the longest of all of Norway's provinces.

THE HIGHLIGHTS: NORDLAND

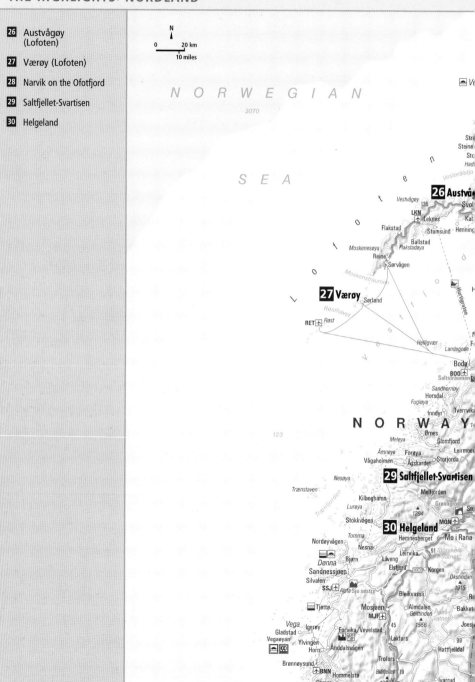

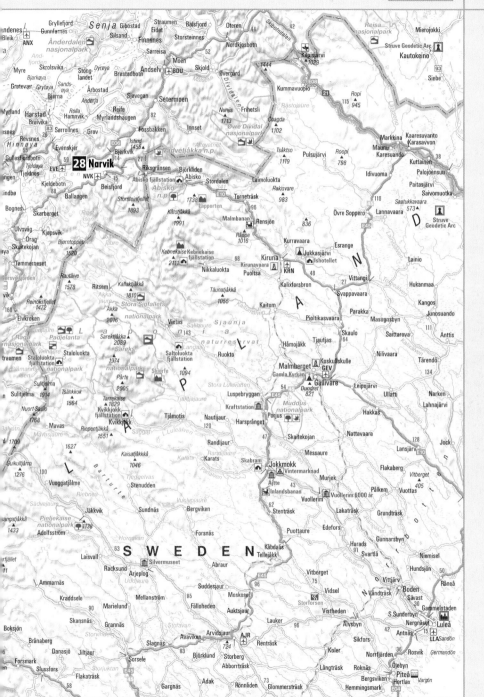

Right: The communities of Reine on Moskenesøya (left) and Henningsvær, the "Venice of the Lofoten", on Austvågøy (right) are the most famous fishing ports in this group of islands. Cod, caught by fishermen in Vestfjord during the winter, is laid out to dry on racks (below).

CENTURIES-OLD TRADITION: KLIPPFISK AND STOCKFISH

Catches of cod and similar fish, as well as of pollock and haddock, were already being salted to preserve them as far back as Viking times. The Vikings also laid fish out to dry in the sun and wind on the cliff tops. This enabled the *klippfisk* ("cliff fish") to be stored for long periods of time, perfect for long sea voyages where it was used as a protein-rich food supply, but the fish was exported as well, particularly during the Middle Ages. In Portugal, for example, this Norwegian fish was used in a national dish known as *bacalhau* which is still eaten today. Stockfish, generally either cod or plaice, is dried on wooden racks in the open air. Traditionally there were five different grades of salt cod, though they are no longer extensively used. Some of the factory-produced lower grades are made by injecting a solution of saltwater into the fish, rather than using dry salt. Stockfish is Norway's oldest sustained export product, also used in the preparation of the traditional Italian dish *stoccafisso* as well as in a variety of other dishes. However, Norway's most famous fish recipe is called *lutefisk*, which is found on the menu of every fish restaurant during Advent. To make it, stockfish is soaked in lye, and then rinsed in water to remove the salt, after which it is boiled. Today, the traditional Lofoten fishing culture of the Vestfjord is under threat: fishing is only permitted here between January and the end of March or beginning of April, while other countries have cod fishing all year round, in addition to farming it.

THE HIGHLIGHTS: NORDLAND

INFO Orca safari

Austvågøy (below) is home to Svolvær, the largest fishing port in Lofoten. Other islands can be found nearby and to the south, such as Flakstadøya (inset below, top) and Moskenesøya, with the small fishing village of Reine (inset below, bottom).

Between October and January, regular safari boats cast off from the Lofoten Islands to follow the orcas. Brave whale watchers can also venture into the water and swim among the gentle giants.
Tysfjord Turistsenter, 8275 Storjord; Tel 75 77 53 70.
www.tysfjord-turistsenter.no

AUSTVÅGØY (LOFOTEN) **26**

The Lofoten archipelago, which is part of the district of Nordland and separates the Vestfjord from the mainland, is in fact a submerged mountain range whose peaks protrude above the sea. The tallest of the peaks are on Austvågøy, the largest island in Lofoten nearly twice the size of New York City at 527 sq. km or 203 sq. miles), where the 1,161-m (3,809-foot) high Higravtin is situated. Viewed from afar, standing alone in the Norwegian Sea, the jagged rock of Austvågøy appears as a single mountain, but in fact the island conceals a variety of landscapes: snow-white beaches, waterfalls, lush valleys, cirques eroded by ice, and valleys, surrounded by mountains sugar-coated with snow. Red wooden houses known as "Rorbu" stand out among the other buildings of the fishing villages. The seven main islands in the Lofoten are: Austvågøy, Vestvågøy, Moskenesøya, Flakstadøya, Værøy, Gimsøy, and tiny Røst.

INFO Bird cliffs

Spectacular: The midnight sun on the Lofoten island of Værøy can be experienced between 30 May and 13 July (right); a hiking trail leads to the top of the island. The 456-m (1496-foot) high Nordlandsnupen is the highest peak on this mountainous island (below), which reaches out into the Norwegian Sea.

Thousands of seabirds also live and breed on the cliffs of Værøy. Boat trips offer a once in a lifetime opportunity to see this amazing sight from close up.

Værøy tourist information can provide details of tours around Måstad and Sørland: Tel 76 09 52 10. www.lofoten.info

The "weather island" of Værøy – so-called because of the rapidly changing microclimate that exists here even in summer – lies in the southern part of Lofoten, near Røst, which has large colonies of seabirds. The Mokstraumen, one of the strongest tidal currents in the world, flows close by. Also known as the "Maelstrom", it was immortalized by the authors Edgar Allan Poe (*A Descent into the Maelström*) and Jules Verne. The trapping of puffins and eagles, which was traditionally the islanders' main source of income, has now become a thing of the past – puffins (*lunde* in Norwegian), jackdaw-like birds that nest among the rocks, have now become a protected species. This has in turn led to the Lundehund, the breed of dog adept at scaling slippery rocks that was used to help hunt the birds, all but dying out, and the bird-hunting village of Måstad now lies deserted. Today, Værøy relies largely on tourism and is accessible by helicopter and boat.

Where the sun (temporarily) never sets: the coastal landscape of Bodø in Nordland by the light of the midnight sun (far right); on Sankt Hans, the Midsummer Night festival on 23 June, everyone likes to dress up for the occasion (right). Flakstad in Lofoten at 1.45 in the morning (below).

U N D E R   T H E   M I D N I G H T   S U N

The land of the midnight sun conjures up a myriad of magical images. In the middle of summer, the sun does not set at all over northern Norway, a phenomenon that can only be experienced north of the Arctic Circle, while the south of the country remains in sunshine for 23 hours. On the North Cape, the sun thrusts the night, the moon, and the stars to one side for around 80 days. The midnight sun is only visible on the actual day of the summer solstice at the Arctic Circle, but the number of days during which the sun is visible increases the nearer you are to North Pole. In Bodø, the largest city in Nordland, the midnight sun can be seen between 4 June and 8 July, and on the North Cape, between 13 May and 29 July. Year after year, millions of people come from all over the world to see this phenomenon and experience the "white nights". During the midsummer festival of Sankt Hans, enormous bonfires (*Sankthansbål*) are lit everywhere and children and adults alike celebrate the beginning of the summer break beneath the midnight sun. In some parts of Norway, mock marriages still take place symbolizing new life, a custom that dates back to the 1800s, though is believed to be even older. The landscape is particularly beautiful at this time of year, but hiking enthusiasts should bear in mind that many of the higher areas within the mountain regions are simply impassable because of melting snow.

THE HIGHLIGHTS: NORDLAND

TIP Fjellheis restaurant

The port of Narvik (below), with its magnificent location and surrounding mountain landscape, is best viewed from the restaurant at the top of the Fagernesfjellet; the cable car continues to run throughout the night in mid-summer (right).

The Fjellheis restaurant on the Fagernesfjellet has a lovely view from a height of 650 m (2,130 feet), and can be reached by cable car.

Fagernesfjellet, 8506 Narvik; Tel 76 94 16 05; opening hours correspond to the cable car journey times: 12.00–1.00 in summer, 13.00–21.00 in winter.

At Narvik on the Ofotfjord (which remains free of ice all year round), the Norwegian mainland is at its narrowest: the Swedish winter sports resort of Riksgränsen is a mere 6.3 km (4 miles) away as the crow flies. The fact that such a narrow area of land reaches heights of 508 m (1,667 feet) has cre- ated one of the most striking stretches of mountain landscape in the north. Here, the European route E10 winds its way northward, and known locally as the Nordkalottvägen, continues toward the ore-mining capital of Kiruna. The Lapland railway line also snakes upward in a heart-stopping series of bends. It is a mining railway whose Norwegian sec- tion (opened in 1902) is known as the Ofotbanen. The Ofotfjord region can also be crossed via the Rallarveien, an old construction road, now used as a cycling and hiking route: on the Norwe- gian section, visitors need a good head for heights. (See also p. 169.)

THE HIGHLIGHTS: NORDLAND

INFO Glacier hikes

Weterdalen, an ice-free valley accessible via a hiking trail, divides Svartisen (right and below) into the separate Vestisen ("west ice") and Austisen ("east ice"). Massive chunks of the glacier disappear as they calve into the Austerdalisen (inset below), swelling the waters of the lake.

The Svartisen glacier can be negotiated by climbers with the aid of ropes, or its bizarre shapes and formations can be explored via ice caverns. Tours take visitors deep into the bowels of the glacier.
Polarsirkelen Reiseliv, O.T. Olsensgate 3, 8602 Mo i Rana; Tel 75 13 92 00.

Saltfjellet-Svartisen on the Arctic Circle is one of Norway's most diverse national parks. Covering an area of 2,102 sq. km (812 sq. miles), it stretches inland from the Nordfjord, where the coastline is warmed by the Gulf Stream. In the center of the park, the Svartisen ("black ice") plateau glacier, at 350 sq. km (135 sq. miles), is the second largest in Norway after the Jostedalsbreen in Vestlandet. East of the glacier, the park continues through the fertile river valleys and glacial high mountain scenery of Saltfjellet. The chalky rock here boasts a thriving, unique variety of flora during the short, intense summer months, and the Sami people have used this area for reindeer migration for thousands of years. The Junkerdal National Park, established in 2004 and also part of Saltfjellet, is close to the Swedish border, and is characterized by a fertile natural landscape and a rich variety of wildlife. Wolverine, moose, and reindeer can be seen here, as well as brown bears.

Right: On the coast within sight of the lighthouse, a monument marks the spot where the European route E6 crosses the Arctic Circle. Fantastic views of the invisible line marking the border between the Arctic and temperate zones are also to be had from on board the Hurtigruten ships (below).

The polar circles have a particular magical resonance all of their own, marking as they do the boundary between the zones that are habitable by humans and those considered inhabitable but which are known for their extremes of climate and light – the Arctic in the north and the Antarctic in the south. The northern Arctic Circle is regarded as the more habitable of the two because of its comparatively milder climate. Unlike the Antarctic, the Arctic is populated in parts (such as by the Inuit and the Sami peoples). In Norway, the boundary marking the limit of human habitation corresponds almost exactly to the northern border of Helgeland and the areas where the Sami live. On the Arctic Circle, at latitude 66° 33' N, on the summer solstice there is clear visibility even in the middle of the night, when the sun remains above the horizon. The phenomenon of the midnight sun can only be experienced north of the Artic Circle. Tour companies providing adventure holidays in the region often include a quasi-mystical-sounding "Arctic Circle baptism" on reaching 66° 33' N, led by a Sami "shaman", who makes the baptismal candidates shiver while he marks their heads with soot. You may even be rewarded with a certificate to commemorate your crossing. Those crossing the Arctic Circle by boat may be in for a different kind of ceremony, involving a crew member dressed up as King Neptune and a celebratory drink.

THE HIGHLIGHTS:
NORDLAND

INFO A living museum

The most powerful currents in the whole of Europe are said to flow through the sound known as Saltstraumen, near Bodø. Torghatten, a 260-m (850-foot) high granite mountain on Torget island near the port of Brønnøysund, attracts many visitors who come to see its 160-m (525-foot) long natural tunnel (below).

The rows of painted houses in historic Sjøgata, part of Mosjøen, the oldest town in Helgeland, act as local landmarks. Sjøgata is effectively a living museum of the 19th century. It also houses many traditional workshops, artisans, and small shops offering typical local products.

Helgeland (literally, "holy land") with its many natural wonders contains some of the most diverse coastal and mountain scenery in Europe. It stretches from the southern coast of Nordland, where there are fjords and islands in their thousands (including the Vega Archipelago, designated a UNESCO World Heritage Site), to the high mountain landscapes on the Swedish border, an area containing the Børgefjell National Park's 1,447 sq. km (559 sq. miles) of wilderness. With the Arctic Circle forming an approximate northern border to the region, Helgeland is the most southerly part of northern Norway. The Hurtigruten ships berth in Helgeland's ports, but visitors exploring by car can make use of the Riksveg 17 that hugs the coast, designated a "National Tourist Route", and the inland E6. The largest town in Helgeland is Mo i Rana on the Ranfjord, situated at the outskirts of the Saltfjellet-Svartisen National Park.

THE HIGHLIGHTS

FINNMARK
AND TROMS

Finnmark and Troms: the Arctic provinces of the Cap of the North (as the landmass north of the Arctic Circle is known), have a total combined surface area greater than that of West Virginia in the USA, but barely a quarter of a million inhabitants. The majority of people are employed by the armed forces or in the tourism sector. The North Cape attracts millions of tourists, and the Alta rock carvings are the artwork of people who lived in the region thousands of years ago. Tromsø is a cultural hub for the province of Troms, while Kirkenes, on the Russian/Finnish border is of great significance historically.

N

0   20 km
    10 miles

N O R W E G I A N

S E A

Loppa
Lopphavet Loppa

Fugløya
Nord-Kvaløy   Vannareid   Årviksand   Sør-Tverrfjor
                Vanna   Arnøy
                              Skardet
Helgøy   Skåningen
Mikkelvik   Storstein   Skjervøy
Rebbenesøy   Hansnes   Russelv   Kågen
Måsvik   Stakkvik   Uløya   Hamneidet
          Ringvassøy   Reinøya.   Sør
                                            Sørkjosen   Storslett
Skulgam   SOJ   Djupvik
Tromvik   Oldervik   1596
          TOS   Breidvikeidet   Svensby   Olderdalen
     Kaldfjord   Ishavskatedralen
Hillesøy   **34 Tromsø**   Forneset   Lyngseidet   Bilto
Laukvik Kvaløya Larseng   Fagernes   66   Kåfjordbotn
Fjordgård   Vikran   1833   EO6   Isfjellet   Mollisi
Bergsfjord   Furuflaten   Skibotn 1375
          Lysnes   Straumen   Stordalselv   Halti
Gryllefjord   Eidet   Balsfjord   42   1365
Andenes   Gunnarnes   **35 Senja** Gibostad   Oteren
Bleik ANX   Finrisnes   Storsteinnes   Nordkjosbotn
36 Vesterålen Åriderdalen   Sørreisa   52   Kilpisjärvi
          nasjonalpark Silsand   1029
Nordmela   And-   Moen
Andøya Myre Skrolsvika Stong- Dyrøya Andselv Skjold Øvergård
              landet   Brøstadbotn BDU
Bjarkøya   Kummavuopio
Risøyhamn Grytøya Sands- Årbostad   21
Grøtevær Bjørna   øya
          Anderja   Sjøvegan Setermoen
Myrland Rolla Reife   Nunjis Frihetsli
Harstad Hamnvik Myrlandshaugen 82   Øvagda
     Breivika   Innset   1713   1102
Flesnes Revsnes Sørrollnes Grov Fossbakken
     Hinnøya Istind 1455
          Evenskjer   Bjerkvik   Tsåktso
Gullesfjordbotn Bogen Narvik Riksgränsen Björkliden   Pulsujärvi
Ladingen Tjeldøya EVE NVK Abisko fjällstation Abisko Stordalen Laimoluokta
Rindbø Kjeldebotn Beisfjord   Abisko 1738   Torneträsk Rakisvare
     Ballangen   Storsteinfjellet   n.p.   983
Bognes   1893   Lapporten
Tranøya Skarberget   Kåtotjåkkå
Ulvsvåg Kjøpsvik   1991 Malmbanan Rensjön 836
Presteid Drag Bjørntoppen   Råppe 1016
Skaitekojan   1520   S W E D E N
Tømmerneset   Købnekaise Kebnekaise   Kurravaara
                        2111 fjällstation 68   Kiruna Jukkasjär
          Rautåive   Nikkaluokta Kirunavaara Ishot
Reinoksfjellet 1578 Ritsem Kallaktjåkkå Puoltsa KRN 48
Mørsvik 1472 Akka 1810   Kalixforsbron
     Elvkroken jaure Stora Sjöfallets Täunatjåkkå Svappava
          Akka   nationalpark   1055
          2016   Kaitum

31 North Cape

BARENTS SEA

Kinnarodden

Knivskjelodden

Magerøya Skarsvåg

Gjesvær 51 **HVG**

Hjelmsøya

Ingøya Honningsvåg

Gunnarnes Havøysund Kjøllefjord

Rolvsøya

Kåfjord

Akkerfjord Repvåg

Snefjord Sværholt-

Porsanger- halvøya

Hammerfest halvøya

HFT

Rypefjord Kvaløya

Kvalsund Russnes

Eidvågeid Olderfjord

Seiland Skaidi

1079

Saraby Indre Billefjord

Nyvoll 88

Storekorsnes **LKL**

Leirbotn Lakselv

Stabbursdalen nasjonalpark

ALF

Alta Porsangermoen

Hjemmeluft Sautso- 1117 73

canyon Jesjavri

N O R W A Y Sápmi

F i n n m a r k s- Karasjok

Masi Kenttan

126 128 Iskaras

542

Biedjovaggigruver Jorgastak

Lappoluobbal v i d d a Gurbbeš

Mierojokki 587

Kautokeino Lavvooaivve

Siebe 622 Øvre Anárjohka

nasjonalpark

Palojärvi Lemmenjoki

Morgam-Viibus

Kaaresuvanto 542

Karasavvon Enontekiö Nunnanen

Enkodak Peltovuoma Lisma

Kuttainen **ENF** Pulju

Palojoensuu Pallas

Paitasjärvi 723

Ounasstunturi Pokka

Saivomuotka Raattama

573 Yli-Muonio 807 Tepasto

Muodoslompolo Muonio Köngäs Kiistala

Särkijärvi

Merasjärvi Kangosjärvi Sirkka Rasti

Lainio Kitkiöjoki

21 **KTT**

74

Kitkiöjärvi Äkäslompolo Kittilä Tepsa

Hukanmaa Kihlanki Jeesiö

Kihlanki Ylläsjärvi Kaukonen Vaalajärvi

Kangos Äkäsjokisuu

asugnsbyn Aareavaara Huuki Alakylä Kierinki Syväjärvi

Junosuando Kurtakko

Gamvik

MEH Mehamn

Nordkinn-

halvøya

Berlevåg

Store Raggonjargga

Molvik

Hopseidet

Veidnes Bekkarfjord 673

Ytre Kjæs Ifjord Rusterfjelbma

Adamsfjord

Børselv *L a k s e f j o r d -*

v i d d a

Rastigaissa 94

1067 Vetsikko

Lævvajokgiedde

101 Utsjoki

Skalltivaara

Nuvvus Patoniva

Guivi Mieraslompolo

641 103

Outakoski Petsikko

Karigasniemi

Kaamasmukka 85 Palomaa

Koarvikodds Kaamanen

590 Mutusjärvi

Inari

Angeli 71

Pyhäjärvi Koppelo

Menesjärvi

Hammastunturi

531 **IVL**

83 Törmänen

Saariselkä

Kuttura

Repojoki S a a r i s e l k ä 718

Tankavaara

Kultamuseo Vuotso

Pomovaara 421

Peurasuvanto 97 Lokka

Petkula

Rasti Tanhua Martti

Tepsa

69 Sattanen

Sodankylä

Aska Kairala Saija

32 Kirkenes

BVG

Båtsfjord

BJF

Sommerset **VAW**

Vardø

Kiberg

V a r a n g e r-

725 *h a l ø y a*

Leirpollskogen Falkefjellet 77

545 **E75**

Vestre **VDS**

Jakobselv Vadsø

Tana bru Varangerbotn 51

V a r a n g e r f j o r d e n

Nuorgam

Polmak Gandvik 111

94 Bugøynes

Bugøyfjord **KKN**

Skoltefossen Bjørnevatn 30

Näätämö

Ahmalahti

Svanvik Salmijärvi

Sevettijärvi Nikel 650

Kobbfoss g.Suort

495

Nyrud

Partakko Prirečnyj

Øvre Pasvik Rajakoski

nasjonalpark Nautsi

119

Virtaniemi

Nellim **R U S S I A**

Ivalo g.Rastimuddar

646

Lotta

Raja- g.Ionn-N'jugoaje

Jooseppi 714

Urho Kekkosen kansallispuisto Korvatunturi

483

F I N L A N D Tulppio

Ruuvaoja

Vintilätunturi

389

Maltiotunturi

478

Savukoski

THE HIGHLIGHTS:
FINNMARK AND TROMS

INFO Sealife safaris

Tens of thousands of visitors flock to the North Cape plateau on the island of Magerøya (right and below) to experience the magical midnight sun during the summer solstice. The E69 leads from Honningsvåg to Porsangerfjord (inset below), and the Nordkapphallen (North Cape Hall) tourist center.

Visitors who are qualified divers can shadow auks (small birds similar in appearance to penguins) underwater as they forage for food. Or stay dry and watch from a boat as birds snatch prey from the sea.
Finnmark Tourist Board,
9509 Alta; Tel 78 44 90 60.
www.finnmark.com

his rocky outcrop of land lying to the orth of Magerøya island at a latitude of 1° 10′ 21″ N, was thought to be the nost northerly point in mainland Europe or centuries – but wrongly so: in fact, his accolade goes to another rocky outrop nearby – Knivskjellodden (see elow), situated at 71° 11′ 09″ N, which stretches 1.5 km (0.9 miles) further north into the sea than the North Cape. Knivskjellodden is not as spectacular however, being much flatter by comparison, while the rocky plateau of the North Cape looms 307 m (1,007 feet) above the Norwegian Sea. When these rocks were first sighted by English explorer Richard Chancellor, chief navigator of the fleet that set off to discover the North-East Passage in 1553, he took it to be the northern apex of the continent and named it the "North Cape". (See also p. 171). The North Cape also marks the point where the Norwegian Sea meets the Barents Sea, north of Russia.

The Northern Lights above the Lofoten archipelago: above Finnmarksvidda and Karasjok (right, from left); in Oslo (below), and on Magerøya island (below right). The Northern Lights appear in all manner of guises: from arcs to radial formations, from flickering flares to luminous clouds that dance like flames.

AURORAS: FAIRY MIST AND DIVINE SIGNS

Ancient accounts ascribe auroras to celestial, mystical, if not magical, sources, while the Viking sagas poetically interpreted them as fairy mist or divine signs. Today, however, science has finally banished such creative attempts at explanation: an aurora, as the decidedly more prosaic version describes it, is a luminous effect created in the night sky by the excitation of oxygen atoms and nitrogen molecules, which can be pinpointed at heights of between 70 and 500 km (45 and 310 miles). The shapes and shades vary, with the most common being green and red arc-like formations. Auroras can appear as the Northern Lights (aurora borealis) or the Southern Lights (aurora australis), and are particularly visible during strong sunspot activity, when particles from the solar winds enter the Earth's magnetic field at the poles, causing the oxygen atoms to emit green and red light, and the nitrogen molecules a weaker blue and violet glow. Auroras appear most often during the winter months. The area where the Northern Lights can be seen stretches like a belt from north Scandinavia across Iceland and the southern point of Greenland, passing over northern Canada, Alaska, and the northern coast of Siberia. Varying levels of solar activity have an effect on the intensity of an aurora and can nudge it toward the equator; on occasion, the Northern Lights have even been observed as far south as the Mediterranean area.

INFO Salmon fishing

Kirkenes (right), situated on the southern arm of the Varangerfjord, is the final port of call for the Hurtigruten ships. As the western part of the Barents Sea only benefits to a limited extent from the warmth of the Gulf Stream, icebreakers are sometimes needed to ensure that the fjord remains passable (below).

Visitors wishing to try their hand at catching salmon from a river – rivers are one of Finnmark's most plentiful sources of fish – can rent equipment and join an expertly led fishing tour on the Neiden River.
Neiden Fjellstue, Øvre Neiden, 9930 Neiden; Tel 78 99 61 41. www.samitour.no

The small port of Kirkenes on the border with Russia and Finland has a deeply symbolic location at the end of the E6 and the Hurtigruten route. It is typical of the mining towns that grew rapidly and then declined between 1906 and 1996, and was named unofficially "the unemployment capital" of Finnmark province when mining came to an end here. Occupied by Germany during World War II, it was the most heavily bombed town in Europe, suffering 320 air strikes. Kirkenes was also seen as a front-line town during the Cold War (located directly on the border between NATO and the Warsaw Pact countries), but later established itself as a service headquarters for the Barents Region, one of the new international cooperation regions set up after the break up of the Soviet Union. Emigration, population decline, and unemployment have prompted calls for the provinces of Finnmark, Troms, and Nordland to be combined. (See also p. 171.)

Reindeer migration early in the year (right and below). Below left, from top: Wedding preparations; cooking over a log fire; the traditional and modern collide – satellite TV and a cast-iron oven sit side by side. Below right, from top: Elaborately costumed – the herd sets off; in front of Kautokeino church; wrapped up tight, even the tiniest soul braves the cold.

THE SAMI: NOMADS FROM THE FAR NORTH

There are around 70,000 Samis, who are indigenous to Lapland. They originally settled further south, but over the centuries retreated into the Cap of the North, away from the warlike Vikings and Finns. The Sami call themselves "Sameks", meaning "marsh people", a name referring to the extensive marshland in the area. They are also known as Lapps in some languages, from the Finnish word *lappi*, meaning people from the "remote place" – from where the UNESCO World Heritage Site of Laponia in Sweden also gets its name. There are around 40,000 Sami living in Norway, 20,000 in Sweden, 7,500 in Finland, and 2,000 in Russia. The criteria used to determine which people are members of this ethnic minority vary from country to country: in Norway, a Sami is someone whose mother tongue is Sami – a Finno-Ugric language related to Finnish – or who can prove Sami ancestry. In 1989, the establishment of the Sameting (the Sami parliament) was an important milestone in recognizing the Sami as an ethnic group. The majority of the Norwegian Sami live in the Finnmarksvidda, with Karasjok as their capital city. A considerable part of the livelihood of around 20 percent of these Sami comes from semi-nomadic reindeer herding. Traditional reindeer herding has been practised by the Sami since the 1700s. They are used for food, clothing, and as working animals, as well as for trade and paying government taxes.

THE HIGHLIGHTS: FINNMARK AND TROMS

INFO Alta Museum

Hjemmeluft in the Altafjord (below) is home to the most important rock carvings north of the Alps. They were carved into the rock around 3000 BC, and depict more than 2,000 elks, reindeer, and other animals (right). In 1985, the Neolithic artworks at Hjemmeluft were designated a UNESCO World Heritage Site.

The museum offers guided tours of the rock carvings, and owns the observatory on the Altafjord.

Altaveien 19, 9518 Alta;
Tel 78 45 63 30; May 8.00–17.00
daily, Jun–Aug 8.00–20.00 daily,
Sept 8.00–17.00 daily, Oct–Apr
Mon–Fri 8.00–15.00, Sat,
Sun 11.00–16.00.

The largest town in Finnmark, Alta is situated at the mouth of one of the finest salmon habitats in the world: the 2,000-km (1,250-mile) long Altaelva River, whose upper reaches are known as Kautokeinoelva, flows from the Sami town of Kautokeino and empties into the Altafjord's many straits and tributaries.

During the summer, the captains of the salmon fishing boats travel upstream in special "river boats" to show the tourists the best fishing grounds. The Altafjord cuts 30 km (18 miles) through Alta's 3,845-sq. km (1,485-sq. mile) community. The Gulf Stream's warming water ensures a mild climate, allowing

birches, alders, aspens, and pines to thrive, thereby encouraging the forestry trade, as well as the cultivation of potatoes and barley. Alta's most important commercial activity is the slate industry: the mining, processing, and export of top-quality Alta slate secures hundreds of local jobs. (See also p. 171.)

THE HIGHLIGHTS: FINNMARK AND TROMS

INFO Polar Museum

The view from Storsteinen over the island city of Tromsø (right), famous for its taverns (inset below, left) and accessible by means of a tunnel and two bridges. The Hurtigruten ships berth at the port (inset below, right). Encircled by mountains and fjords, Tromsø experiences spectacular light conditions (below).

In a warehouse dating from 1830, this museum provides information about life in the extreme north.

Søndre Tollbodgt 11,
9259 Tromsø; Tel 77 60 66 30;
1 Mar–15 Jun 11.00–17.00, 16
Jun–15 Aug 10.00–19.00, 16
Aug–30 Sept 11.00–17.00,
1 Oct–28 Feb 11.00–16.00.

Sometimes known as the "Paris of the North", Tromsø, capital of Troms province, is northern Norway's largest city with 62,000 inhabitants. Situated in the extreme north-west of the country among a group of islands protected by the Gulf Stream, the climate is relatively mild for its northerly location. When this small settlement of 70 people was elevated to city status in 1794, it sparked rapid development, and Tromsø soon become a commercial cathedral city – and the "capital" of the Arctic Ocean. Tromsø also gained renown as the starting point for Arctic expeditions – the Polar Museum documents the expeditions of the great explorer Fridtjof Nansen, among others. The city's research facilities boost the economy, and the university hospital is the largest employer for some miles. A monorail takes visitors up the nearby Mount Storsteinen (420 m/1,378 feet), from where there is a magnificent view. (See also p. 170.)

INFO Panoramic route

"The Devil's Teeth" (Djevelens Tanngard, below left) are a legendary collection of rock formations on Senja's weather-eroded coastline, situated in the fjord landscape of the Ersfjord (right), Mefjord (below middle), and Øyfjord, whose final branch ends in Husøy (below right).

Visitors wanting to see the most impressive view across this richly contrasting landscape should take a trip along the National Tourist Route that runs between Gryllefjord and Laukvik, seemingly inextricably entwined with these coastal fjords. *Information: Tel 81 52 20 00. www.turistveg.no*

Covering some 1,586 sq. km (612 sq. miles), Senja is the second largest inland island in Norway, after Hinnøya in the nearby Vesterålen archipelago. The weather-beaten coastline with its jagged fjords ranks as one of the most wild mountain and coastal landscapes in the north. The peaks of its rock forma-tions tower out of the surf at heights ranging from 500 m (1,600 feet) to almost 1,000 m (3,280 feet). The south of the island is lush and green. Ånderdalen National Park was opened in 1970 and enlarged to 125 sq. km (48 sq. miles) in 2004. Many visitors are attracted by its lakes – which are rich in fish – its water-falls, and its dense woodland – which contains giant conifers up to 500 years old. The Hulder- og Trollparken (Hulder and Troll Park) is a theme park that owes its existence to the trolls that also inhabit the island; the Senja Troll, almost 18 m (59 feet) high, holds every troll world record going. (See also p. 170.)

THE HIGHLIGHTS:
FINNMARK AND TROMS

Blooming willowherb transforms the fen landscape of the Vesterålen islands into a sea of pink. The inspiring mountain scenery in the south (below) takes most visitors' breath away. Langøya is home to the fishing village of Nyksund, abandoned in 1972 (right).

INFO Whale watching

During the summer, the sea around Andenes becomes one of the sperm whale's most popular haunts. Whale-watching trips are on offer daily – there is a 95 percent chance of actually spotting whales.
*Hvalsenter Andenes;
Tel 76 11 56 00.
www.whalesafari.com*

The island chain of Vesterålen stretches for more than 150 km (93 miles) along the Troms coastline, merging almost seamlessly into the Lofoten archipelago further south – the narrow Raftsund Bridge over to Trollfjord on the Lofoten side marks the boundary between them. The two island groups also boast similar landscapes: Vesterålen is home to fjords, straits, inlets, skerries, rivers, lakes, plateaus, fens, and valleys, as well as Alpine-like peaks and sandy beaches. The chief islands are Hinnøya (Norway's largest inland island, covering 2,205 sq. km or 851 sq. miles), Langøya, and Andøya. The year 2003 saw the creation of the Møysalen National Park in Hinnøya, which covers 51 sq. km (20 sq. miles) and includes Møysalen (1,266 m/4,154 feet), the highest peak in the Vesterålen islands. Despite being so close, only part of Hinnøya belongs to the province of Troms, with the rest forming part of Nordland. (See also p. 170.)

Right, from left: A plethora of shapes and shades – a spring anemone; a fly orchid; and an uncurling frond. Wind and weather, together with the natural landscape, leave their mark on the rich Norwegian plant life that exists between fjord and fjell, a particular feature of the national parks (below).

A VARIETY OF PLANT LIFE

Norway's geographical shape may be slender, but it makes up for its lack of girth with its mountainous profile. The west, which benefits from the warm currents of the Norwegian Sea, is decidedly different to the east, which joins the rest of the continent. This contrast can be seen in the plant world's enormously rich variety of species – such as in the fjells, the uncultivated mountain landscapes found above the alpine tree line. The fjells are split into three distinct vegetation zones. The lowest is the so-called "willow belt" containing the Lapland, Purple Osier, and Cotton varieties of willow among others, as well as forests of fjell birches that grow up to 12 m (39 feet) high, and cold-resistant deciduous trees such as aspens and mountain ashes. The fjells also boast lush bushes and shrubs. The fens and heaths are typically home to bakeapples, cottongrass, dwarf birches, heather, and dwarf shrubs. The willow belt, which has increased rapidly in size over the course of the 20th century, rises to 1,500 m (4,900 feet) in Jotunheimen. The vegetation zone above it is dominated by grasses and grass-like plants. The point where this continuous belt of vegetation dwindles to mosses and lichens clinging to weathered stone is known as the high mountain belt. The alpine tree line varies dramatically in height: in Østlandet in eastern Norway, it stands at around 900–1,100 m (3,000–3,600 feet), whereas in the north it sinks to sea level.

THE HIGHLIGHTS

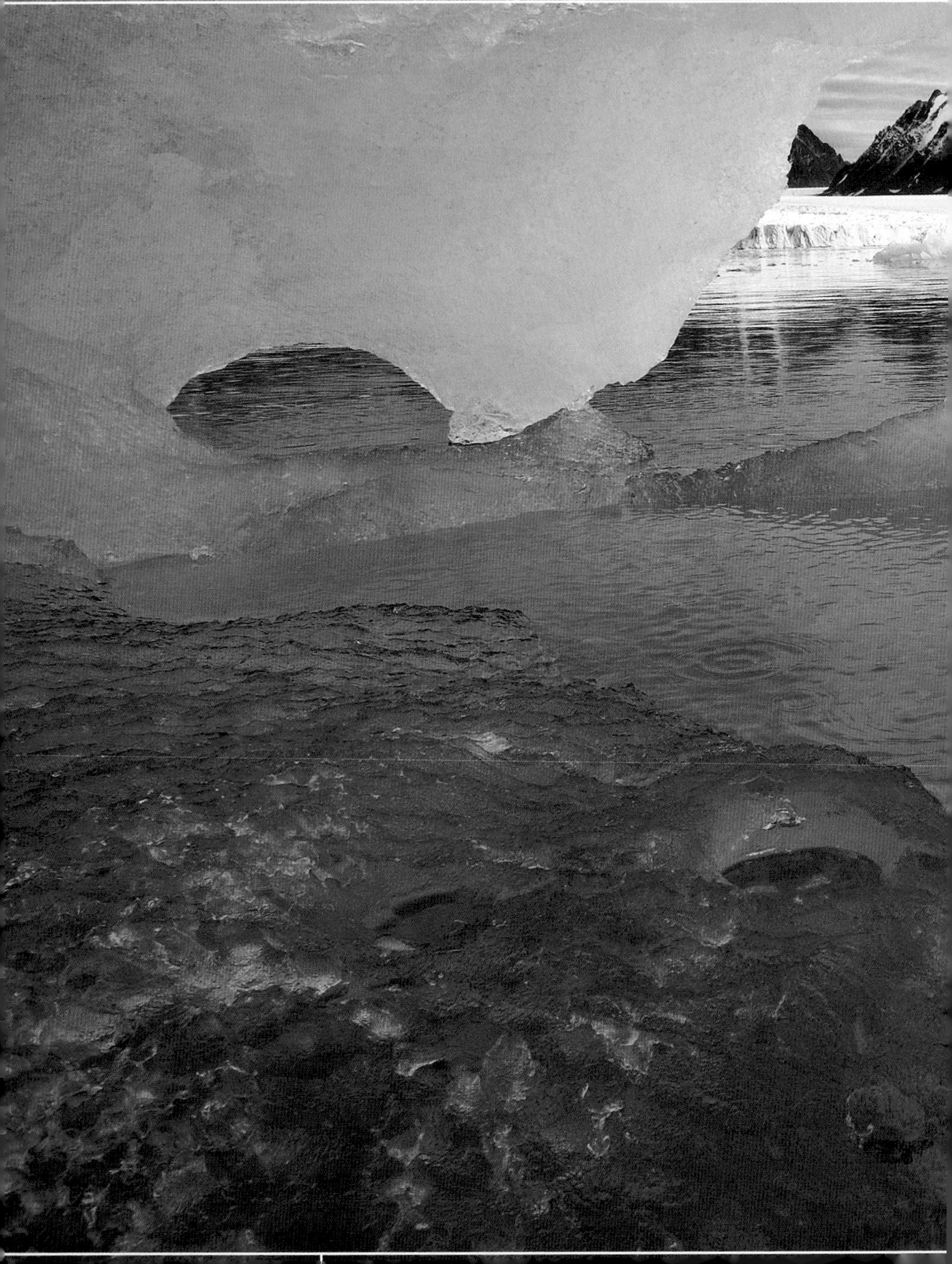

SVALBARD

In 1194, the Vikings landed on a group of islands that they named "Svalbard" (literally, "cold shores"). This name now refers to the Norwegian administrative district, made up of ten larger islands and numerous smaller ones, which is situated around 600 km (370 miles) north of the mainland. Over half of the archipelago's 61,000 sq. km (23,500 sq. miles) is covered with glaciers. The principal town, and the local seat of administration, is Longyearbyen on Spitsbergen – the largest island in the group (a similar size to Switzerland) and the only one to have been continuously inhabited. The name Spitsbergen is occasionally used to refer to the whole Svalbard archipelago.

37 Spitsbergen

38 Jan Mayen

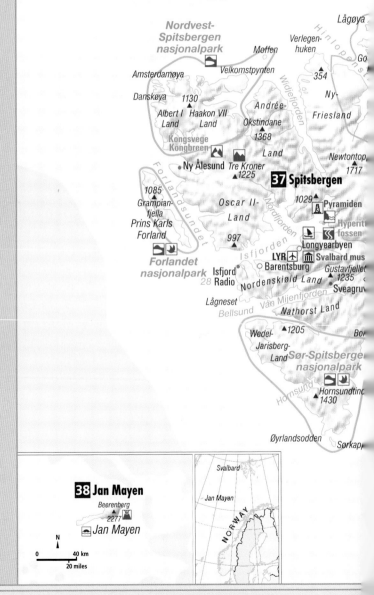

iuøyane
øya *Martensøya*   Karl XII-øya   Foynøya   Kvitøya   ▲410

Nordenskiold-   *Repøyane*   **Nordaust-**
ppen   *bukta*   607▲   Storøya   **Svalbard**
v v Land   *Orvin Land*   **naturreservat**

Nordaust-Svalbard   *Austfonna*

nna   *Isispynten*

N o r d a u s t l a n d e t

erg- ▲   *Sørfonna*   *Abeløya*
340   **naturreservat**   *Kongsøya*
                                                              Rivalensundet
/on Otterøyane   *320*
Wilhelmøya   *230*
                                    Svenskøya   **Nordaust-**
Kapp Payer   **Svalbard**
                                    Kapp   **naturreservat**
                                    Hammerfest **Kong Karls Land**

Haastberget   **Barentsøya**

665 **Søraust-** *Kapp Heuglin*   **S v a l b a r d (N)**
Freemansundet   67

Svalbard   *Ryke*
590   **Edgeøya**   *Yseøyane*
naturreservat

Kvalpynten   *395*   *Halvmåneøya*
Tusen-   ▲
øyane
                              Beisaren
Håøya
                    Hopen
          Hopen Radio *Kapp Thor*   103
                    370

B A R E N T S   S E A

N
0   40 km
20 miles

Because of their limited facial expressions, polar bears are notoriously unpredictable: visitors should keep well away – polar bears often attack without warning. To intimidate their opponents, they rear up onto their powerful hind legs, particularly when fighting off other males during the mating season.

POLAR BEARS: DANGEROUS AND ENDANGERED

Polar bears, Arctic foxes, and Svalbard reindeer are Svalbard's most important land mammals. The polar bear (Ursus maritimus) is closely related to the brown bear, and its habitat has only fairly recently (in geological terms) been limited to the Arctic coast and the drift ice at its edges – from about 50,000 years ago. Their thick, almost completely white, water-repellent fur allows these fine swimmers and divers (they can hold their breath for up to two minutes) to blend almost entirely into the surrounding landscape. These huge solitary mammals, up to 2.5 m (8.2 feet) long, are almost exclusively carnivorous and eat mainly seals, fish, and seabirds, supplemented by plants during the short summer. An exceptionally keen sense of smell also allows these bears to hunt seals inside ice caves. For thousands of years, the polar bear's only notable enemy has been man: along every Arctic coast, men have hunted polar bears for their tasty meat and their warm fur, used to make coats. In the 19th and 20th centuries, trophy hunters (who hunted from ships and aircraft, and rigged spring guns on the ice) had a devastating effect on polar bear numbers, until the international Oslo Agreement made the hunting of polar bears illegal in 1973. Nowadays, the bears face the dangers posed by pollution and climate change instead. Malnutrition or starvation due to the loss of habitat and food supply through global warming is now the main threat.

THE HIGHLIGHTS: SVALBARD

INFO Walking tours

The peaks and fjords of Spitsbergen promise magnificent views across the Arctic surroundings, overlooking Magdalena Bay (below), Hornsund (right), and Raudfjord in the midnight sun (below right, top). Icebergs and pack ice in the Arctic Ocean (below right, bottom).

The Longyearbyen tourist office offers a wide choice of organized tours. However, it is dangerous for visitors to venture off on their own – and not just because of the likelihood of meeting a polar bear.
Svalbard Reiseliv, 9171 Longyearbyen; Tel 79 02 55 50. www.svalbard.net

Thanks to Svalbard's location around 1,200 km (750 miles) south of the North Pole, the climate of these islands is distinctly Arctic. The combination of glaciers, ocean straits full of drift and pack ice, and a yearly average temperature of –5 °C (23 °F), means that Spitsbergen is only sparsely populated, mostly by Norwegians and Russians working in the coal mines (such as the one in Barentsburg), as well as the international teams manning the weather and climate research stations in Ny-Ålesund. The Arctic landscape's harsh beauty is thanks to its craggy coastline of fjords, such as Isfjord, Kongsfjord, and Hornsund, as well as the up to 1,700-m (5,600-foot) high "pointed peaks" (as "Spitsbergen" translates), which prompted explorer Willem Barents to give the island its current name in 1596. Various expeditions have set off from Longyearbyen to explore the rich array of wildlife (including polar bears, as well as numerous types of seals and whales) that lives in this island world, the majority of which is designated a national nature park. (See also p. 172.)

TIP Island contact

Beerenberg (or Haakon VII Toppen) at the northern end of Jan Mayen is the most northerly volcano in the world (below). It was last active in 1985, and the main crater is 2 km (1.2 miles) across. The igneous rock beneath the endless fields of ice shapes the landscape (right).

In principle, tourists are allowed to visit Jan Mayen, but in practice they meet with a variety of difficulties since the island has neither a port nor a commercial airfield. The island's website provides information on (and a link to) a company that organizes excursions: *www.jan-mayen.no*

The glacial volcanic island of Jan Mayen is situated in the Greenland Sea area of the North Atlantic Ocean, about halfway between Iceland and Spitsbergen. In 1929, Norway took control of this island – named after the Dutch whaler Jan Jacobszoon May, and covering an area of around 377 sq. km (146 sq. miles) – in order to establish a further base for the whaling industry. Lichens and mosses grow on the igneous rocks, but otherwise the vegetation on the island is sparse. Thanks to the warming Gulf Stream, the water temperature averages +1° C (34 °F), and even the average annual air temperature is relatively high at −1.4 °C (29.5 °F). There is no port due to the dangerous cliffs, only offshore anchorages, and the "resident population" consists of the crew of the radio and weather station, who are flown in and out by means of a small airfield. Normally numbering around 18, the population doubles in summer. (See also p. 173.)

NORWAY EXPLORER

COMPACT NORWAY

Whichever part of Norway you visit, evidence of this Scandinavian country's rich cultural heritage is never far away. An old seafaring nation, Norway's maritime past is impressively documented in many of its museums. There are a particularly large number of open-air museums, showcasing traditional customs and building methods. Norway's national parks, meanwhile, are spread across the entire country, providing a safe haven for its flourishing flora and fauna. There's also a huge range of outdoor activities on offer, and the country's unspoiled countryside, superb skiing areas, and salmon-rich rivers all appeal to lovers of the great outdoors. The road network is excellent. Many of the country's fjords can be crossed by ferry, while scheduled cruise liners – an increasingly popular way of visiting more than one destination while on one vacation – serve key ports.

Stavanger

(See p. 20.)

🔲 Nordialog Stavanger
This is the place to buy the latest in information technology. Mobile phones (especially Scandinavian models), computers, and software are the top sellers.
Hillevågsveien 24;
Tel 51 90 60 00;
Mon–Fri 8.00–16.00.
www.nordialog.no

🔲 First Hotel Alstor
This thoroughly stylish hotel is one of Stavanger's best. There are 31 comfortable rooms. The Restaurant Rossmann serves Norwegian and international dishes.
Tjensvollveien 31;
Tel 52 04 40 00.
www.firsthotels.com/alstor

Klosterøy

🏛 Utstein Kloster (Monastery)
This Augustinian monastery is located on the island of Klosterøy, north-west of Stavanger. Dedicated to St Laurence, the monastery is superbly preserved, and its rich history is told in the monastery museum. The monastery also serves as a concert venue.
Tel 51 72 47 05;
Tues–Sat 10.00–16.00,
Sun 12.00–17.00.
www.utstein-kloster.no

Haugesund

🔲 Haraldshaugen
This imposing monument to Norway's legendary medieval king Harald Hårfagre (Harald Fairhair) lies about 2 km (1 mile) north of Haugesund. Harald is believed to be buried here, and the 17-m

(56-foot) tall obelisk that marks the spot can be seen from far and wide. This national monument was erected in 1872 to commemorate the 1,000th anniversary of Norwegian unification, and the 29 stones surrounding the obelisk represent the 29 regions Harald united. You can visit the monument all year round, and it makes a good focus for a walk through the local area.
Turistinformasjon,
Karmsundsgaten 51;
Tel 52 01 08 20.
www.visithaugelandet.no

❎ Bestastuå
Mat Prat & Vinhus
This excellent restaurant occupies an historic building in the middle of Haugesund, and has its own piano bar and nightclub, separate from the main dining area. You'll find superb Norwegian and international dishes on the menu, and some fantastic paintings – mostly depicting Norway's spectacular landscape – on the walls. After dinner, retire to the bar for a complimentary cognac.
Strandgata 132;
Tel 52 86 55 88;
Mon–Thurs 12.00–1.30, Fri,
Sat 13.00–3.30.
www.bestastua.com

Sauda

🔲 Sauda Skisenter
Sauda Ski Center is situated 5 km (3 miles) outside Saudasjøen. It is one of the biggest in south-west Norway, offering perfect conditions for downhill, cross-country, and snowboarding. The downhill runs are up to 6 km (4 miles) long, while the cross-country tracks lead deep into the surrounding forests. Some

stretches are lit at night. Families will appreciate the good range of organized activities for children, and the après-ski scene is also lively. A shuttle bus service provides a convenient connection to Sauda, the nearest town.
Tel 52 78 56 56;
Tues, Thurs, Fri 10.00–20.00,
Wed, Sat, Sun 10.00–16.00.
www.saudaskisenter.no

Rosendal

🏛 Baroniet Rosendal
With its small, renaissance castle, this noble estate dates back to 1665. It is one of the most popular tourist attractions in Vestlandet, and home to a sizeable art collection that includes paintings, tapestries, and porcelain. The courtyard is the venue for occasional concerts and theatrical performances, while the picturesque landscaped grounds – complete with rose garden and several pavilions – are perfect for a nice stroll. Poised between the mountains, the Baroniet became a popular subject of Norwegian Romantic painting. For a look inside, join one of the guided tours.
Tel 53 48 29 99;
hourly guided tours May,
Jun 11.00–15.00 daily,
Jul, Aug 10.00–17.00 daily,
Sept 12.00 daily.
www.baroniet.no

Sørfjord

🔲 Walking
The banks of the 38-km (24-mile) long branch of the Hardangerfjord make beautiful hiking territory. Spectacular waterfalls are just some of the attractions along the way – notably the 103-m (338-foot) high Tveitafossen that

marks the beginning of the route. From here, and the nearby hydroelectric power station, the walk continues to the Sotefossen and Nykkjesoyfossen. Thanks to the spray from the waterfalls, the plant life in this area is lush. There is a thick layer of moss across the rock faces, and a thick covering of lichen on the tree trunks. It takes about four hours to get back to the beginning of the walk, but it's worth taking a detour into the small village of Lofthus – in the spring, it's surrounded by tens of thousands of blooming fruit trees. The Hardangervidda – Scandinavia's biggest mountain plateau – stretches out to the east of the Sørfjord. (See p. 26.)

Voss

🏛 Folkemuseum
This open-air Folk Museum has been a guardian of the traditional way of life around the fjords since its foundation in 1928. Its wooden buildings date from the 17th to the 19th centuries, and bear witness not only to old-fashioned building methods, but also to the daily routine of the people who lived in them. Tools, furniture, pictures, and photographs are amongst the exhibits.
Mølstervegen 143;
Tel 56 51 15 11;
Mid-May–mid-Sept
10.00–17.00 daily,
mid-Sept–mid-May Mon–Fri
10.00–15.00, Sun
12.00–15.00.
www.vossfolkemuseum.no

🏛 Vossajazz
Norway is famous for its many musical events, and the Vossa jazz jazz festival – which takes place at the beginning of Apr

Views of Vestlandet (from left): Utstein Monastery; on the Lysefjord in Stavanger; the Flåm line, Flåm, is the world's steepest railway; Baroniet Rosendal, an elegantly furnished country manor; and Atlantic puffins on Runde.

VESTLANDET

These pages give additional information for the area described in the "Highlights" chapter (pp. 16–49).

– is one of the first important dates in the country's musical diary. There are several stages dotted across the town, attracting both Norwegian artists and international bands. There's also a strong focus on world music, with performances by artists from all over the globe.
Tel 56 52 99 11.
www.vossajazz.no

Flåm

🎬 The Flåm Railway
The journey from the edge of the Aurlandfjord at Flåm to the mountain station at Myrdal is one of Europe's most scenic railway trips, and the line has long been one of Norway's biggest tourist attractions. Excluding cog railways, it is also the world's steepest railway, and the train climbs some 864 m (2,835 feet) over its 20-km (12-mile) long route. The journey takes about an hour, during which time passengers are treated to spectacular, panoramic views of snow-capped mountains, rushing waterfalls, dense forests, lush green meadows, and – of course – the fjord itself. The train also travels through no less than 20 tunnels. There are nine or ten services a day between May and September, and four a day during the winter.
Tel 57 63 14 00.
www.flaamsbana.no

Bergen

🏨 Hammam Spa
Hydrotherapy, different types of massage, and specialist skin care are just some of the treatments available at Bergen's biggest wellbeing spa. Alongside traditional treatments, the

spa also offers aromatherapy and Ayurveda. Guests can enjoy the use of the pool, Jacuzzi, and sauna.
Nedre Ole Bulls plass 4;
Tel 55 96 14 40;
Tues–Sat 10.00–20.00,
Mon 12.00–18.00.
www.hammamspa.no

🛍 CityBag Bryggen
Alongside the briefcases, travel bags, wallets, and other leather goods, this shop also stocks typically Norwegian souvenirs and handicrafts, including troll figurines, glassware, and porcelain.
Bryggen 9; Tel 55 31 83 90;
Jul, Aug 8.30–22.30 daily,
Sept–Jun Mon–Fri
10.00–17.00 (Thurs until
19.00), Sat 10.00–15.00.

🏨 Steens Hotel
Located right on the waterfront, the hotel occupies an elegant villa that dates from 1890. With its 21 beautifully furnished guest rooms, the hotel decor is impressive. The dining room – complete with tapestries, wood panels, and chandeliers – is particularly inviting.
Parkvei 22; Tel 55 30 88 88.
www.steenshotel.no

Runde island

🎬 Birdwatching
Take a ferry or fast boat from Ålesund to reach the birdwatcher's paradise that is Runde. Over 200 species of bird have been spotted on this rocky island, foremost among them the Northern Gannet, Black-legged Kittiwake, Common Guillemot, Northern Fulmar, and Atlantic Puffin. The cliffs are about 200–300 m (656–984 feet) high, and are easily climbed –

paying attention, of course, to the strict conservation rules. The island covers an area of 6 sq. km (2 sq. miles). To see the whole island take a round trip by boat.
www.rundecentre.no

Ålesund

(See p. 47.)

🏛 Ålesund Museum
The town museum houses a wide variety of collections. The history of the town, and of the local shipbuilding and fishing industries, are just three areas on which the museum is particularly strong. One of the most interesting sections of the museum is its collection of art nouveau objects, but there are also natural history displays – including one about the Arctic.
Rasmus Rønnebergsgate 16;
Tel 70 12 31 70; Feb–Mar
Mon–Fri 11.00–15.00,
Apr–mid-Jun Mon–Fri
9.00–15.00, Sat 11.00–15.00,
Sun 12.00–15.00, mid-
Jun–Aug Mon–Fri
9.00–16.00, Sat 11.00–15.00,
Sun 12.00–16.00, Sept–Dec
Mon–Fri 11.00–15.00.
www.aalesunds.museum.no

❎ Fjellstua
The oldest restaurant in town towers over it from the top of a cliff, a dizzying 130 m (427 feet) above sea level. Even the shortest path from the coast is a 418-step climb, but the amazing panoramic view you'll get from the restaurant's terrace is well worth the effort. On the menu, you'll find a wide range of Norwegian and international fish and meat dishes, as well as a tempting selection of homemade desserts.
Aksla; Tel 70 10 74 00;

Feb–Apr, Oct–Dec
11.00–16.00 daily, May
11.00–18.00 daily, Jun, Aug
11.00–20.00 daily, Jul
10.00–22.00 daily, Sept
11.00–17.00, daily.
www.fjellstua.no

Molde

🏛 Bjørnson Festival
Molde's literary festival has been held every August since 1992. The event is named after the Norwegian writer and Nobel Prize winner Bjørnstjerne Bjørnson, who spent his childhood here. It features readings, art exhibitions, and workshops.
Sandvegen 4;
Tel. 71 25 80 98.
www.bjornsonfestivalen.no

🛍 Eventyrlige Skaret – Lysgården
Lysgården (the candle maker's) has a candle for every occasion. This charming shop sells candles in every size, shape, shade, and scent – all made in its own workshop. There's also a range of candlesticks and other accessories.
Lysgården, Molde;
Tel 71 26 80 97.
www.skarstua.no

🏨 Fjordstuer
As well as its 11 spacious guest rooms, this hotel also boasts seven apartments that are ideal for a longer stay. The hotel has two restaurants: the ever popular Fjordstua fish restaurant, and – down on the quayside – Løkta. Both provide a good vantage point from which to watch the passing Hurtigruten ferries and fishing boats.
Julsundveien 6;
Tel 71 20 10 60.
www.classicnorway.no

Larvik

📧 **Hotel Wassilioff**
Named after its original owner, the Hotel Wassilioff first opened for business in 1844. There are 47 guest rooms, all individually furnished, and some with views of the Skagerrak strait. The hotel restaurant is among Larvik's finest, serving a wide range of tempting fish dishes.
Havnegate 1; Tel 33 11 36 00. www.wassilioff.no

Sandefjord

ℹ️ **Tourist information**
Despite its modern appearance, Sandefjord's long history as a place of both settlement and trade is betrayed by archeological finds that lead all the way back to Viking times – including a complete ship discovered here in 1880. Sandefjord was once an important spa town, its mud baths frequented by members of the Norwegian royal family. The spa closed in 1939, and until 1968 whale fishing was the cornerstone of the local economy – a chapter of Sandefjord's history that is recorded in the Hvalfangstmuseet (whale-fishing museum).
Sandefjord Turistkontor, Thor Dahlsgate 7; Tel 33 46 05 90; Jul–mid-Aug Mon–Fri 9.00–18.00, Sat 10.00–16.30, Sun 12.30–16.30, mid-Aug–Jun Mon–Fri 9.00–16.00. www.visitsandefjord.com

Tønsberg

📧 **Active Cabin Hotel AS**
Opened in 2006, this fresh and comfortable hotel successfully combines its warm decor with a real sense of maritime style. Its 46 simply furnished rooms

have all the essentials covered, while the food at the Ocean Point restaurant demonstrates the many flavours of Scandinavian cuisine. Guest can use the adjacent fitness facilities.
Stalsbergveien 5; Tel 33 34 59 10. www.cabin.no

Horten

ℹ️ **Horten Kommune**
Horten is a popular stop for sailors, who moor at the port and enjoy a short stay in this small town. Characterized by its old wooden houses, the central part of town has retained its 19th-century charm. The Royal Norwegian Navy Museum (Marine-museet) and the Photography Museum (Preus Museum) are the cultural highlights.
Apotekergaten 12; Tel 33 08 50 00. www.horten.kommune.no

Skien

🏛️ **Henrik Ibsen Museum**
This southern Norwegian town is perhaps best known as the birthplace of Norway's greatest writer – born here in 1828. The Ibsen Museum, founded in 1958, is housed in the farmstead occupied by Ibsen and his parents from 1835–43, and the building's dingy loft room assumed a central role in Ibsen's play *The Wild Duck*. There is a wide range of exhibits relating to the great dramatist, who died in 1906.
Venstøphøgda 74; Tel 35 52 57 49; Mid-May–Aug 10.00–18.00 daily. www.telemark.museum.no

🏛️ **Telemark Museum**
This open-air museum takes in the entire cultural spectrum of

the Telemark area. Set within Brekke Park, the museum's 14 buildings display local customs, traditional crafts, and folk art – including rose painting, woodcarvings, and jewelry – alongside exhibitions of modern art. Several rooms are devoted to the dramatist Henrik Ibsen, while parts of the grounds – landscaped in the English style – serve as a botanical garden. The vivid hues of the tulips are particularly splendid.
Øvregate 41; Tel 35 54 45 00; Museum: May–Aug Mon–Fri 12.00–18.00, Sat, Sun 12.00–18.00 Park: May–Aug Mon–Fri 11.00–22.00, Sat, Sun 11.00–24.00. www.telemark.museum.no

📧 **Clarion Collection Hotel Bryggeparken**
Many of this excellent hotel's 103 guest rooms look out over the water. A whirlpool, sauna, and steam bath are just some of the creature comforts on offer, and the hotel also has its own restaurant and cocktail bar. The clean lines of designer furniture set a stylish tone.
Langbryggen 8; Tel 35 91 21 00. www.choicehotels.no

Ulefoss

🎭 **Telemark Canal**
The 105-km (65-mile) long Telemark Canal is one of Norway's most important waterways, both as a tourist attraction and in terms of its wider economic significance. One of the most attractive stretches – best negotiated by canoe – leads inland from Ulefoss, passing through forests and rocky terrain. The stretch begins at the bottom of an 11-m (36-foot) high

waterfall. The Ulefoss Sluser – a three-step, staircase lock that is still hand-operated – allows you to get to the top.

Notodden

ℹ️ **Notodden Kommune**
As its industrial museum explains, Notodden grew up around the sawmills and industrial workshops that originally operated here. The rose painting that adorns the houses is particularly noteworthy, and the annual Blues festival – held every August – is renowned across Europe. Outside Notodden itself, Heddal stave church – a short distance to the west of town – is the main attraction.
Teatergata 3; Tel 35 01 50 00; Sept–mid-May Mon–Fri 8.00–15.30, mid-May–Aug Mon–Fri 8.00–15.00. www.notodden.kommune.no

Kongsberg

🏛️ **Norsk Bergverksmuseum**
The Norwegian Mining Museum is one of Kongsberg's biggest attractions. There was a working silver mine here until 1957, and the exhibition explains the unforgiving task of extracting the silver ore. In the 18th century, as many as four thousand miners were employed here. Today, you can get into the tunnel system by mine train, but the 5-km (3-mile) walk through the mine is even more exciting.
Hyttegata 3; Tel 32 72 32 00; tours mid-May–Jun 11.00, 13.00, and 15.00 daily, Jul–mid-Aug 11.00, 12.00, 13.00, 14.00, 15.00, and 16.00 daily, mid-Aug–end Aug 11.00, 13.00, and 15.00, daily. www.bvm.museum.no

Nordic culture, and relaxation (from left): a trip on the Telemark Canal; the Norwegian Mining Museum in Kongsberg; a shop in the Norsk Folkemuseum; and in the Hadeland glassworks.

ØSTLANDET

These pages give additional information for the area described in the "Highlights" chapter (pp. 50–75).

Oslo

(See p. 60.)

🏛 Fram Museum

The museum's name gives away the identity of its star attraction, namely the *Fram* – the famous ship used by both Fridtjof Nansen and, later, Roald Amundsen in their respective explorations of the North Polar Sea and Antarctic. The *Fram* was the only ship of its time to venture so close to the North and South Poles, and the museum explores the entire history of Norwegian polar exploration. There's another of Amundsen's vessels - the *Gjøa* – on display outside.
Bygdøynesveien 36;
Tel 23 28 29 50; Nov–Feb
Mon–Fri 10.00–15.00,
Sat, Sun 10.00–16.00, Mar,
Apr, Oct 10.00–16.00 daily,
May, Sept 10.00–17.00 daily,
Jun–Aug 9.00–18.00 daily.
www.fram.museum.no

🏛 Norsk Folkemuseum

The Norwegian Museum of Cultural History is Europe's largest open-air museum. Opened in 1894, its 150 buildings are set over 14 ha (35 acres). The farm reconstructions – complete with furniture, tools, and people dressed in traditional costume - recreate the working and living conditions of a bygone era. Don't miss the medieval stave church.
Museumsveien 10;
Tel 22 12 37 00;
Mon–Fri 11.00–15.00, Sat,
Sun 11.00–16.00.
www.norskfolke.museum.no

🏛 Norsk Sjøfartsmuseum

Right on the waterfront, the Norwegian Maritime Museum truly lives up to its name. The museum documents the entire history of man's seafaring enterprise, from primitive dugout all the way to the very latest modern ship. Numerous model ships help tell the story, and whole sections of the display are devoted to specific topics like marine archeology, fishing, and shipbuilding. Visitors can also view a film journey along the Norwegian coast.
Bygdøynesveien 37;
Tel 24 11 41 50;
Mid-May–Aug 10.00–18.00 daily, Sept–mid-May 10.30–16.00 daily (Thurs until 18.00).www.norsksjofartsmuseum.no

🧖 Creative Wellness Center

Whether you want to be pampered all day, or just recharge your batteries between sightseeing tours, this is the place to experience all the latest wellness treatments.
Drammensveien 159;
Tel 23 25 36 30; Mon–Fri 9.00–18.00, Sat 9.00–15.00.
www.creative-wellness.no

🔱 Juhls Silvergallery

Norwegian craft doesn't get much more authentic than this unique, Arctic-themed jewelry on sale here. The chains, bracelets, pendants, and brooches are all produced in workshops in Lapland.
Roald Amundsens gate 6;
Tel 22 42 77 99; Mon–Sat 9.00–18.00. www.juhls.no

Jevnaker

🔱 Hadeland Glassverk

The Hadeland glassworks were founded in 1762, and the company is the oldest glass producer in Norway. As well as buying glass, visitors to the factory can also watch the glassblowers at work, and learn more about their craft from the accompanying exhibition. Children's workshops at weekends and during vacations give kids the chance to blow their own glass, or try their hand at candle making. It really is a family-friendly attraction.
Jevnaker; Tel 61 31 64 00;
Mon–Fri 10.00–17.00, Sat 10.00–16.00, Sun 11.00–17.00.
www.hadeland-glassverk.no

Hamar

🏛 Norsk Jernbanemuseum

Founded in 1896, this is one of the oldest railway museums of its kind in the world. The museum's grounds include Norway's oldest railway building, and its exhibition halls tell the complete history of Norwegian rail transport. The country's largest steam locomotive always pulls in the crowds.
Strandveien 132;
Tel 62 51 31 60;
Mon–Sat 11.00–15.00, Sun 11.00–16.00, except Jul–mid-Aug 10.00–17.00 daily.
www.jernbanemuseum.no

🏛 Vikingskipet Olympic Arena

This arena, on the eastern bank of Lake Mjøsa, has become a symbol of the town. Its spectacular roof is reminiscent of an upturned Viking ship. It was the venue for the speed skating in the 1994 Winter Olympics, and now hosts concerts and other events.
Åkersvikveien 1;
Tel 62 51 75 00; www.hoa.no

Gjøvik

🏨 Thon Hotel Gjøvik

The hotel is located right in the heart of Gjøvik, and boasts fantastic spa and fitness facilities. There are 83 attractively furnished guest rooms, and an excellent restaurant.
Stradgaten 15;
Tel 61 13 20 00.
www.thonhotels.com/gjovik

Lillehammer

(See p. 68.)

🏛 Norges Olympiske Museum

A stone's throw from the Lillehammer ski jump, the Norwegian Olympic Museum documents the sporting history of the Olympics. It's also a chance to relive the atmosphere of the Lillehammer Winter Olympics, held here in 1994.
Tel 61 25 21 00;
Jun–Aug 10.00–17.00 daily, Sept 11.00–16.00 daily, Oct–May Tues–Sun 11.00–16.00.
www.ol.museum.no

🏨 Birkebeineren Hotel & Apartments

This attractive, red wooden building is located right in the heart of Lillehammer's Olympic park, and its 40 apartments and 48 guest rooms are all well equipped. There's no restaurant, but you can use the barbecue.
Birkebeinerenveien 24;
Tel 61 26 47 00;
www.birkebeineren.no

Fåberg

🎡 Hunderfossen Familiepark

Rafting down a tempestuous artificial river is one of the most thrilling rides at this family theme park. There's also a troll park, waxworks display, adventure ship, and all manner of rides.
Tel 61 27 55 30; Jun–mid-Aug 10.00–17.00 daily, Jul 10.00–19.00.
www.hunderfossen.no

Flekkefjord

ℹ️ Hollenderbyen

The Hollenderbyen, Flekkefjord's attractive Dutch quarter, lies just north of the middle of town. Its narrow, winding lanes are flanked by white wooden houses dating from the 18th century. Back then, timber and granite were shipped from this small port all the way to the distant Netherlands.
Flekkefjord Kommune;
Tel 38 32 80 00;
Mon–Fri 8.00–15.30.
www.flekkefjord.no

ℹ️ Hidra island

The small island of Hidra is a ferry ride from Flekkefjord, and its fjord landscape provides a variety of interesting walks. The coastline is very steep in places, but the view of the sea and mainland is impressive. It's a popular destination for anglers and nature lovers alike.

🏛️ Flekkefjord Museum

The museum's collection of furniture and textiles helps to recall the daily lives of the people who lived here in the 18th century. There are also a small number of special collections on topics including prehistoric life or the hard daily routine of local seamen. It's all housed in a listed building that dates from the 18th century.
Dr. Krafts gate 15–17;
Tel 38 32 81 40;
mid-Jun–Aug Mon–Fri
12.00–17.00,
Sat, Sun 12.00–15.00.
www.flekkefjordmuseum.no

🛏️ Grand Hotell

Built in 1897, the Grand Hotell – with its characteristic bay windows and small turrets – is surely one of Flekkefjord's most attractive buildings. The rooms are comfortably furnished, and many have a balcony overlooking the sea. The hotel restaurant serves mostly Scandinavian cuisine.
Anders Beers gate 9;
Tel 38 32 53 00.
www.grand-hotell.no

Mandal

(See p. 82)

ℹ️ Tourist information

Mandal is best known for the nearby Sjøsanden beach, which is widely held to be one of Norway's finest. But the town itself has retained more historic buildings than you'll find in many other places along the country's southern coast. The church, completed in 1821, is one of the biggest in Norway, and can accommodate a congregation of 1,800. The annual August shellfish festival – at which the finest seafood delicacies are served on a 100-m (330-foot) long table – is also famous across the whole of Norway.
Bryggegata 10;
Tel 38 27 83 00.
www.mandal.kommune.no

Lindesnes

(See p. 80.)

🛏️ Lindesnes Camping og Hytteutleie

Norway's southernmost camping site is located around 3 km (2 miles) from Cape Lindesnes, the southernmost point of the Norwegian mainland. It is one of the nicest camping sites in the area – ideally placed right on the coast and perfect for anyone who just wants to get out into nature. The site is very well equipped, and you can sleep in either a tent or – for full sanitary facilities and other mod cons – in one of the cabins. Bikes and boats are available for hire.
Lillehavn, Spangereid;
Tel 38 25 88 74.
www.lindesnescamping.no

Øyslebø

🎣 Salmon fishing in Mandal River

The rivers of Sørlandet are famed for their rich stocks of fish, and salmon fishing in the river Mandal attracts large numbers of anglers. The river is practically overflowing with salmon for nearly 50 km (31 miles); in many places you don't need to wade too far in to find them – making the Mandal especially suitable for beginners. You can book a guided tour of the fishing grounds at various points along the river.

Kristiansand

(See p. 82)

🏛️ Kristiansand Domkirke

Kristiansand's neo-Gothic cathedral was completed in 1885. It is the third church to stand on the town's market square, its predecessors both having been destroyed by two major town fires. Eilif Petersen's altarpiece, which shows Christ at Emmaus, is one of the decorative highlights. Climb the tower for a fantastic view over the town.
Gyldenløvesgate 9;
Tel 38 19 69 00;
Jun–Aug Mon–Fri
9.00–14.00; tower Jul
Mon–Sat 11.00–17.00.
www.kristiansand.kirken.no

🏛️ Kristiansand Dyrepark

Around 10 km (6 miles) east of Kristiansand, this zoo and amusement park is a top family attraction. The park spans an area of some 600,000 sq. m (148 acres), surrounded by countryside. There are elk, wolves, monkeys, zebras, and giraffes, as well as a water park and a fantastic recreation of the town featured in the much loved Norwegian children's story *When the Robbers Came to Cardamom Town* – a dramatised version of which is staged here in summer.
Kardemomme By;
Tel 38 04 97 00;
Mid-Jun–mid-Aug
10.00–19.00 daily,
mid-Aug–mid Jun
10.00–15.00 daily.
www.dyreparken.no

❌ Sjøhuset Restaurant

This former salt warehouse was built in 1892. It is right on the waterfront, and the restaurant's seafood dishes could hardly be any fresher. Time your meal carefully, and you'll also get to enjoy the sunset from the large terrace. The menu gets pricier in the evening, so an afternoon fish platter is the cheaper option.
Østre Strandgate 12a;
Tel 38 02 62 02;
Mon–Sat 15.00–23.00.
www.sjohuset.no

🛏️ Sjøglott

This small, family-run hotel is a good choice for visitors on a budget. All the rooms feature bathroom, television, and wireless internet access, and the freshly baked bread served at breakfast is said to be the best in town.
Østre Strandgate 25;
Tel 38 70 15 66.
www.sjoglott.no

From left: Nature, effortlessly beautiful and serene in summer; fall on the river Otra at Evje; a house facade in Flekkefjord; Kristiansand Zoo and Amusement Park; and holiday accommodation in Lyngør.

SØRLANDET

These pages give additional information for the area described in the "Highlights" chapter (pp. 76–86).

Vennesla

🚉 Setesdalsbanen
Here's an attraction to get railway enthusiasts' pulses racing. Seated in one of the lovingly restored carriages, this is a chance to enjoy a trip under a glorious full head of steam. The narrow-gauge line was in regular service from 1896–1962. Today, the smoke from the old-fashioned engine serves as a last reminder of a happier, less hectic era.
Grovane stasjon;
Tel 38 15 64 82;
departures mid-Jun–Aug
Sun 11.30, 13.15, 15.10, Jul
also Tues–Fri 18.05.
www.setesdalsbanen.no

Lillesand
(See p. 82)

ℹ️ Lillesand Kommune
Many of Lillesand's old wooden houses have been painted a gleaming white. In the 19th century, the town's thriving shipbuilding industry powered an economic boom that lasted until the decline of the sailing ship around 1900. This proud chapter of Lillesand history is told by its maritime museum. In the Høvåg district, meanwhile, you can see the remains of a bronze age settlement.
Østregate 2; Tel 37 26 15 00.
www.lillesand.kommune.no

Grimstad

❌ Haven Brasserie
Opened in 2001, the Haven Brasserie serves Norwegian cuisine alongside classic Italian pizzas and pasta dishes. You can't fail to be impressed by the waterside location and view of Grimstad port, and the good children's menu makes it particularly suitable for families.
Storgata 4; Tel 37 04 90 22;
from 14.00, daily.
www.havenbrasserie.no

🛏️ Rica Hotel Grimstad
Occupying an attractive wooden building, the Rica Hotel positively exudes maritime flair. Its 98 rooms are furnished in Scandinavian style, and boast unusually spacious bathrooms. Down on the ground floor, the pleasant atmosphere of the Kjeller'n restaurant attracts more than a few locals.
Kirkegaten 3; Tel 37 25 25 25.
www.rica-hotels.com

Arendal

🏛️ Aust-Agder Kulturhistoriske Senter
Located on the northern edge of Arendal, this is one of Norway's oldest museums. It focuses on the history, culture, and traditional customs of Aust-Agder province. Two of the most interesting sections are the archeological collection and the maritime display. There are also sections covering local crafts, furniture, and traditional Norwegian costume.
Parkveien 16;
Tel 37 07 35 00;
Jul–mid-Aug Mon–Fri
9.00–17.00, Sun 12.00–17.00,
mid-Aug–Jun Mon–Fri
9.00–15.00, Sun 12.00–15.00.
www.aaks.no

❌ Madam Reiersen
There's a wide range of international dishes – including low-calorie choices – on the menu of this restaurant, but you'll get an equally warm welcome even if you only want a drink. Talented local jazz musicians play live on Saturday afternoons, and the music takes a country and western turn on Mondays.
Nedre Tyholmsvei 3;
Tel 37 02 19 00;
Mon–Fri 11.30–2.00, Sat
11.00–2.00, Sun 14.00–2.00.
www.madamreiersen.no

🛏️ Clarion Hotel Tyholmen
This award-winning, central Arendal hotel has 60 guest rooms, many of which offer a superb view of the Skagerrak strait and the beautiful sandy beaches of coastal islands like Hisøy and Tromøy. Whether you're staying in the old wooden building or the 2007 extension, you'll enjoy spacious rooms, top-notch service, and numerous amenities.
Teaterplassen 2;
Tel 37 07 68 00.
www.choicehotels.no

Tvedestrand

ℹ️ Tourist information
Tvedestrand is a popular base for holidaymakers. The infrastructure is excellent, and there's a wide choice of holiday apartments and houses. Stroll through central Tvedestrand, and you'll notice the countless antiquarian bookshops – stocking over 300,000 books between them. Out on the edge of town, meanwhile, some of the Sørlandet region's characteristic farms have been preserved. In July, visitors flock to the annual Tvedestrand regatta.
Tvedestrand Turistkontor,
Fritz Smiths gate 1;
Tel 37 16 11 01.
www.tvedestrand.
kommune.no

Lyngør

ℹ️ Tourist information
The painted house fronts of the idyllic village of Lyngør are spread across four islands off the east coast. Entirely free of cars, it can only be reached by boat. As a weekend and holiday destination, Lyngør is particularly popular with visitors from in and around Oslo. It falls within the Tvedestrand Kommune.
Tvedestrand Turistkontor,
Fritz Smiths gate 1,
Tel 37 16 11 01.

Risør

🛶 Havpadlern
If you need something for your kayak, or, in fact, any conceivable type of canoe, this is the place to find it. There's everything from boats and paddles to specialist clothing, safety devices, and navigational instruments. You can also hire a boat and sign up for one of the store's organized canoe tours and courses. You can enjoy a guided paddling tour around Risør or take one of the many classes on offer, which cater for different levels of experience and those with special needs. Tailor-made packages are available.
Fie; Tel 91 32 71 33.
www.havpadlern.no

🛏️ Risør Hotel
Parts of the hotel building date back to 1861, and even those that don't are furnished in the style of that period. The Inger Johanne Mat & Vinstue restaurant serves a good selection of fish and meat dishes.
Tangengata 16;
Tel 37 14 80 00.
www.risorhotel.no

Oppdal

🏛 Oppdal Bygdemuseum
There are some 30 different buildings in the Oppdal open-air museum, including houses, stables, storerooms, mills, a forge, and a classroom. But displays of textiles and tools, as well as the exhibition of skis and skiing equipment from the 19th century to the present day are also well worth a look.
Museumsveien;
Tel 72 40 15 10;
Jul–mid-Aug Tues–Sun
(by appointment)

🏊 Oppdal Skisenter
Winter sport enthusiasts flock to the Oppdal skiing area, which is one of the biggest in Norway. There are around 200 km (124 miles) of ski and snowboarding slopes, as well as plenty of cross-country ski tracks. The floodlit slopes are especially popular, with some stretches open until 20.00. Equipment can be hired on the spot.
Tel 72 40 10 00; mid-Nov–25 Dec 10.00–15.00 daily, 26 Dec–Apr 10.00–16.00 daily.
www.oppdal.com/no/vinter

🛏 Quality Hotel Oppdal
This is one of the biggest hotels in central Norway. Of its 75 rooms, 18 feature a four-poster bed. Thanks to the good transport links to the skiing area, it's especially popular with skiers. The hotel has several restaurants. The Perrongen serves hearty steaks and pasta dishes, while the Gourmetstuen appeals to a more sophisticated palate.
O. Skasliens vei 8;
Tel 72 40 07 00;
www.oppdalbooking.no/ho

Røros

(See p. 100.)

🏛 Olavsgruva (Olav's Mine, part of Rørosmuseet)
The mines to which Røros owes its current economic significance now lie still, but you can get a good idea of what conditions in a copper mine used to be like from Olav's Mine, east of Røros. In summer, concerts are held in the Bergmannshallen. Here, 500 m (1,640 feet) into the mountain, the temperature is a constant 5°C (41°F) all year round. The extensive cave system can be viewed by joining one of the guided tours.
Located 13 km east of Røros; Tel 72 40 61 70; guided tours Jun–mid-Sept daily, mid-Sept–May Sat 15.00. www.rorosmuseet.no

🏛 Rørosmuseet
The Smeltery uses 1:10 scale models to illustrate the techniques once used underground to mine for ore. The buildings in which this informative museum is housed have been reconstructed using traditional, local building methods.
Malmplassen;
Tel 72 40 61 70; Jun–Aug 11.00–16.00 daily, check website for rest of year (heritage events in summer).
www.rorosmuseet.no

🏊 Forollhogna National Park
This 1,513-sq. km (584-sq. mile) area was declared a national park in 2001. The highest point of the plateau is, at a height of 1,332 m (4,370 feet), Mount Forollhogna. Numerous endangered plant species are among the park's lush vegetation. There are hiking paths throughout the park, and these also lead to some of its lakes. Reindeer herds are a not uncommon sight along the way.
Johan Falbergets vei 16, Røros;
Tel 72 41 00 00;
Mon–Fri 8.00–15.30.
www.forollhogna.org

✕ Vertshuset Røros
Vertshuset serves breakfast, lunch, and dinner – as well as afternoon coffee and cake. There's an unmistakable taste of the Mediterranean to many of the dishes, and the list of fine wines leaves nothing to be desired. You can sometimes catch live jazz in the bar.
Kjerkgata 34;
Tel 72 41 93 50;
Mon–Fri 7.00–22.00, Sat, Sun 8.00–22.00.
www.vertshusetroros.no

🛏 Bergstadens Hotel
The hotel has 90 pleasantly furnished rooms, all equipped with a television, radio, telephone, and minibar. There are two hotel restaurants and four bars. Popular with golfers planning to play the course just 11 km (7 miles) down the road, the hotel also has its own sauna.
Osloveien 2;
Tel 72 40 60 80.
www.bergstaden.no

Trondheim

(See p. 96.)

🏛 Ringve Museum
Opened in 1952, the Ringve is Norway's national museum of music and musical instruments. Some 1,800 exhibits from all over the world are on display. The collection uses the instruments and extensive accompanying information to introduce visitors to individual composers from different periods. A special section is devoted to Norwegian folk music.
Lade Allé 60; Tel 73 87 02 80;
mid-Apr–mid-May Mon–Fri 11.00–15.00, Sun 11.00–16.00, mid-May–mid-Sept 11.00–15.00 daily, except Jul, Aug 11.00–17.00, mid-Sept–mid Apr Sun 11.00–16.00.
www.ringve.com

🏊 Pirbadet
Norway's biggest indoor swimming attraction has plenty to keep swimmers busy. There's a 50-m (164-foot) pool in which to swim lengths, and, for the more adventurous, a separate diving pool, as well as a further pool equipped with an artificial wave machine. There's also a whirlpool and waterslide. A large sauna area completes the package.
Havnegata 12;
Tel 73 83 18 00;
Mon, Wed, Fri 6.30–21.00, Tues, Thurs 12.00–21.00, Sat, Sun 10.00–19.00.
www.pirbadet.no

🛍 Solsiden
This waterfront shopping mall is a shopper's paradise. With 57 specialist shops selling fashion, design, necklaces, glassware, sports equipment, and more, as well as 12 cafés and restaurants, you won't have any trouble at all spending half the day here – if no longer. While parents do the rounds of the shops, kids can make the most of Norway's largest covered playground.
Beddingen 10; Tel 73 60 10 00; Mon–Fri 10.00–21.00, Sat 10.00–18.00.
www.solsidensenter.no

This landscape defies all the usual clichés (from left): On the Namsen near Grong; close to nature in Forollhogna National Park; a coffee break in Trondheim; and boats in Grong.

TRØNDELAG

These pages give additional information for the area described in the "Highlights" chapter (pp. 90–105).

☒ Mojo Tapas & Cocktail

Spanish cuisine has well and truly arrived in the northern hemisphere, and this restaurant has a great selection of tapas. It's also the home of Trondheim's best cocktails, and there's no beating the Mojo barmen when it comes to thinking up new ones. A wide selection of Iberian wines is also available. A live DJ takes to the decks on Fridays and Saturdays.
Nordre gate 24;
Tel 73 60 06 40;
Mon–Thurs 16.00–24.00,
Fri, Sat 16.00–3.00.
www.mojo.no

☒ To Rom og Kjøkken

With an emphasis on fish and seafood, it's the quality of the Mediterranean-inspired menu that makes this restaurant stand out. After dinner, cocktails at the bar come highly recommended. Occasional cookery courses and wine-tasting sessions take place on the second floor.
Carl Johans gate 5;
Tel 73 56 89 00;
Mon–Thurs 16.00–1.00,
Fri, Sat 16.00–2.00.
www.toromogkjokken.no

⬛ Clarion Collection Hotel Bakeriet

With wireless internet access in each of its 109 guest rooms, you won't have any trouble keeping in touch with the outside world at this hotel. That said, the Turkish bath and Finnish sauna are the ideal way to relax after a sightseeing tour of Trondheim. As the name suggests, the hotel is in a former bakery.
Brattorgata 2;
Tel 73 99 10 00.
www.choicehotels.no

⬛ Scandic Solsiden

This large hotel close to the middle of Trondheim has 155 guest rooms. Facilities are excellent all round, including those for business. The hotel restaurant serves a good selection of international dishes, and a children's playroom is available in the summer. It also has its own car park.
Beddingen 1;
Tel 21 61 46 00.
www.scandichotels.com

⬛ Thon Hotel Trondheim

The hotel's central location means venues, restaurants, and shops are all close at hand. Though it doesn't have its own restaurant, the hotel does offer an impressive buffet breakfast. The 115 rooms are decorated to a high standard. Good value for money.
Kongens gate 15;
Tel 73 88 47 88.
www.thonhotels.com/trondheim

Levanger

ℹ Levanger Kommune

Levanger has traditionally been an important agricultural area, and its many farmsteads exhibit the long farmhouses that are typical of the region. Central Levanger is characterized by its wood buildings, constructed after a major fire in 1897. The annual Levanger martnan, a market that takes place in August, dates back to the 15th century. Not far south of Levanger, the stone church of Alstadhaug is even older – it was built in 1150, and its impressive frescoes date from the 13th century.
Tel 74 05 25 00.
www.levanger.no

Stiklestad

ℹ Stiklestad Kommune

This is one of the most historically significant places in the whole of Norway. In 1030, it was the scene of the defining battle that sealed the country's Christianization. This Viking battle is re-enacted every year on 29 July. The church is among the village's most interesting buildings.
Tel 74 04 42 00.
www.stiklestad.no

Steinkjer

☒ Mitt Hjem

The menu here is mostly composed of familiar steak and pasta dishes, but what really attracts many of Mitt Hjem's customers is its atmosphere and cozy bar. There's no drink the bar staff can't rustle up, and there's sometimes live music, too.
Steinkjer; Tel 95 23 83 70;
Tues–Thurs 17.00–23.00, Fri,
Sat 16.00–2.00, Sun
13.00–22.00.
www.mitthjem.as

⬛ Tingvold Park Hotel

The Tingvold Park Hotel was built on the remains of an old Viking wall in 1892, and has retained much of its original 19th-century style. This sense of elegance is also visible in the decoration of the 53 guest rooms, and the whole building has recently been renovated.
Gamle Kongeveg 47;
Tel 74 14 11 00.
www.tingvoldhotel.no

Namsos

ℹ Namsos Kommune

Characterized by its many wooden houses, Namsos was founded in 1845 as a port of lading for timber shipments. It is also the point at which the river Namsen, the longest river in Trøndelag, flows into the sea. One of Norway's richest salmon rivers, the Namsen is a popular destination for anglers.
Tel 74 21 71 00.
www.namsos.kommune.no

Grong

⬛ Namsen Laksavarium

The first tourists arrived in Grong around 1800. They were hobby fishermen, and there was one fish they wanted to catch more than any other: salmon. Today, Norway's biggest salmon aquarium is home to many different specimens of this prized fish, in all its various sizes – and visitors can even try their luck at catching one. There's a buffet offering delicious salmon (what else!) in the adjacent restaurant.
Tel 74 31 27 00;
Jun, Aug 11.00–17.00 daily,
Jul 10.00–18.00 daily.
www.namsenlaksavarium.no

Namsskogan

⬛ Namsskogan Familiepark

There's something for the whole family at this zoo and leisure park, where visitors come face to face with elk, reindeer, deer, bears, and other Scandinavian wildlife in their natural habitat. You can also venture out onto the lake in a canoe, or take a thrilling ride down the summer bobsleigh track.
Tel 74 33 37 00;
Jun–Aug 10.00–18.00 daily.
www.namsskogan-familiepark.no

Brønnøysund

Hildurs Urterarium

Just north of Brønnøysund, Hildurs Urterarium is home to a varied and fragrant herb garden, as well as numerous rose bushes and cacti. It also has its own art gallery and a farm shop selling herbs, souvenirs, and homemade wine. Phone in advance to book a guided tour, including the opportunity to sample some of the local delicacies.
Tel 75 02 51 34.
www.urterariet.com

Torghatten

Setting out from Brønnøysund, take a boat trip to the island of Torget to reach the foot of Mount Torghatten. The walk up to the 258-m (846-foot) high summit takes about 30 minutes. The curious hole in the side of the mountain is around 30 m (98 feet) deep, and is believed to have been created through erosion of the lower rocks by the crashing sea. A whole panoply of legends have grown up around Torghatten, and it is these that have really made it famous. The magnificent view of the craggy island landscape you'll get from the top of Torghatten is another reason to make the effort of climbing it.

Galeasen Hotell AS

The Galeasen enjoys an ideal portside location, and many of its 22 comfortably furnished rooms come with a sea view. All feature internet access, television, and telephone. The hotel also has its own restaurant, and you can dine on the terrace in the summer.
Havnegata 34;
Tel 75 00 88 50.
www.galeasen.com

Rødligården

This friendly hotel's nine rooms range from singles to spacious family accommodation. Though simply furnished, all come with a television and internet access. The hotel restaurant, Klara & Alfred, serves plain, unpretentious dishes and tempting cakes. Alternatively, you can even use the hotel's kitchen to prepare your meals yourself.
Havnegata 29;
Tel 97 40 80 00.
www.rodligarden.no

Trofors

Storforsen Camping

If getting close to nature is your thing, this campsite fits the bill. Its 20 cabins each sleep four people, and are equipped with cooking facilities, fridge, and coffee machine. There's also a communal barbecue. The largely unspoiled countryside around Trofors offers plenty of excellent walks, as well as numerous places to go fishing – including along the salmon-rich Laksfossen River.
Tel 41 28 43 59

Mosjøen

Vefsn Museum

Mosjøen has retained many of its old wooden buildings, and the 12 that make up this museum provide a real insight into the lifestyles and traditional building methods of the 18th and 19th centuries. The accompanying exhibitions of contempory art offer a chance to become familiar with the Nordland modern art scene.
Austerbrygdveien 2;
Tel 75 11 01 00;
Tues–Fri 10.00–15.30.

Sandnessjøen

Tourist information

Sandnessjøen lies on the island of Alsten. The port is served by Hurtigruten ships, and the 1,073-m (3,520-foot) long Helgelandsbrua, a bridge that connects the island to the mainland. Alsten's main attraction is a range of seven mountains known as the Sjv Søstre (Seven Sisters). The individual mountains are Botnkrona, Grytfoten, Skjæringen, Kvasstinden, Breitinden, and Tvillingene – the latter accounting for two of the seven peaks. Reaching an altitude of some 1,000 m (3,280 feet), they are easily accessible from Sandnessjøen, and can be climbed without the need for any specialist equipment.
Sandnessjøen Turistinformasjon, Torolv Kveldulvsons gate 25a; Tel 75 04 45 00.
www.helgelandskysten.com

Mo i Rana

Grønligrotta

Located north of Mo i Rana, this cave is one of Nordland's biggest tourist attractions. Here, the limestone landscape that dominates the region has been formed into all sorts of weird and wonderful shapes by the river. The 1,200-m (3,937-foot) long cave network contains some incredible stalactites and stalagmites, and is illuminated throughout. Visitors are led through the cave on guided tours. The route through the cave is quite demanding. Be prepared to get a little wet.
15 Jun–20 Aug 10.00–19.00 daily, tours hourly on the hour.

Restaurant Babettes

From meat and fish to pizza, pasta, burgers, and crunchy salads, you're sure to find something you fancy on this menu. The meat and fish dishes are also available from the barbeque. Alternatively, pop in for a cup of tea or coffee and a piece of cake. If the weather's nice, you can sit on the terrace.
Ranheimgata 2,
Tel. 75 15 44 33;
Mon–Sat 11.00–24.00, Sun 13.00–23.00.
www.restaurant-babettes.no

Meyergården Hotell

Built in 1890 and completely refitted in 1991, this is one of the region's oldest hotels. It boasts 150 guest rooms spread over five floors, and amenities include a sauna and health club. Diners in the hotel restaurant are treated to a variety of regional dishes, and the menu also features a wide selection of reindeer meat dishes.
Fridtjof Nansens gate 28;
Tel 75 13 40 00.
www.meyergarden.no

Rogdan

Salten Museum

This open-air museum contains a range of buildings dating from the 17th to the 20th centuries, all of which stand on the so-called "museum path". They include barns, a bakery, and a school. Also on show is the cabin from Sir Ernest Shackleton's polar exploration ship, the Quest.
Prinsengate 116;
Tel 75 50 35 00;
mid-Jun–mid-Aug 11.00–17.00 daily.
www.saltenmuseum.no

With its tranquil islands, this is a place of splendid isolation (from left): The island of Vestvågøy in Lofoten; a small wooden church in Flakstad; the beach on Flakstadøya; and decorative glass from Vikten.

NORDLAND

These pages give additional information for the area described in the "Highlights" chapter (pp. 106–125).

Bodø

🏛 Norsk Luftfartsmuseum
The National Norwegian Aviation Museum brings the country's aviation history to life, covering both civil and military air transport. Among the biggest attractions are an American spy plane, several seaplanes, a helicopter, and a flight simulator.
Olav V gate;
Tel 75 50 78 50;
Mon–Fri 10.00–16.00, Sat, Sun 11.00–17.00 (mid-Jun–mid-Aug until 18.00).
www.luftfart.museum.no

🎨 Husfliden
If you're on the lookout for original Norwegian crafts, Husfliden is a good place to start – from knitted and woven goods to wooden items, decorative glass, necklaces, bracelets, and ceramics, it's all here in abundance! Souvenir hunters beware – choosing a memento of your trip won't be easy!
Storgata 15; Tel 75 54 43 00;
Mon–Fri 9.30–17.00 (Thurs until 18.00), Sat 10.00–15.00.
www.norskflid.no/bodo

☒ Bryggerikaia
Famed for its superb Norwegian cuisine, Bryggerikaia is one of the most celebrated restaurants in town. There's a view of the sea from the terrace and, in the summer, dining out here is hard to beat. On Friday and Saturday evenings, you'll also find some of Norway's best cocktail pianists tickling the ivories in the adjoining piano bar.
Sjøgaten 1;
Tel 75 52 58 08;
Mon–Sat 11.00–3.30, Sun 12.00–3.30.
www.bryggerikaia.no

☒ Kafé Kafka
Named after the writer Franz Kafka, this café near the port is a Bodø institution. If the bookshelves on the walls are a little reminiscent of a library, then it's a library with real atmosphere, and it's not uncommon to see customers perusing a book over their meal or coffee. On the menu, you'll find unpretentious mains – jacket potatoes, for example – and homemade cakes.
Sandgata 5v;
Tel 93 40 60 03;
Mon–Thurs 11.00–24.00, Fri, Sat 11.00–1.00.
www.kafka.no

🛏 Bodø Hotell AS
This cozy, family-run hotel's 31 guest rooms are furnished in typical north Norwegian style. All feature parquet flooring, a comfy seating area, cable TV, radio, and telephone. There's also a sauna.
Prof. Schyttesgate 5;
Tel 75 54 77 00.
www.bodohotell.no

Kjerringøy

🏛 Kjerringøy Handelssted
This open-air museum is the perfect place in which to learn about the culture of northern Norway. In an idyllic setting, the Kerringøy Trading Post consists of 15 buildings, all dating from the 19th century, many with their original contents. A 20-minute slide show acts as an introduction to the museum and there are guided tours around the buildings. There is also a shop and a café.
Tel 75 50 35 00;
mid-May–Aug 11.00–17.00 daily, Sept Sun 11.00–17.00.
www.saltenmuseum.no

Narvik

(See p. 118.)

🏛 Ofoten Museum
The museum documents the history of Narvik and the surrounding area. There's a particular emphasis on the importance of the town's port, which is ice-free all year round. It is from here that iron ore mined in the Swedish city of Kiruna is exported all over the world.
Administrasjonsveien 3;
Tel 76 96 96 50;
Mon–Fri 10.00–15.00, Jul–mid-Aug also Sat, Sun 12.00–15.00.
www.ofoten.museum.no

🛏 Nordstjernen Hotell
This good value hotel has its own restaurant and 24 nicely furnished rooms and suites.
Kongensgate 26;
Tel 76 94 41 20.
www.nordstjernen.no

Flakstad

ℹ Flakstad Kommune
The municipality of Flakstad includes the entire island of Flakstadøya and part of Moskensøya. The majority of the inhabitants live in the towns of Fredvang and Ramberg, the administrative capital. Ramberg's wooden church was built in 1870. It is topped with an onion-shaped dome, and boasts a painted pulpit. The fishing village of Nusfjord is another attraction. It is one of the best-preserved villages in the entire Lofoten region, and enjoys protected status on the UNESCO World Heritage list. Flakstad's pottery and the glass factory in Vikten are also popular tourist destinations.
Ramberg;
Tel 76 05 22 01.
www.flakstad.kommune.no

Vestvågøy

ℹ Vestvågøy Kommune
Meadows with grazing cows are the overriding image of Vestvågøy Kommune, which includes Vestvågøy, the second largest of the Lofoten islands. Broad swathes of agricultural land are framed by mountains that rise up to approximately 1,000 m (3,280 feet) above sea level. Stunning, long beaches run along the north coast, while on the south coast, Stamsund is the main hub of western Lofoten's transport infrastructure, and a port of call on the Hurtigruten line. In Borg, the Lofotr Viking Museum brings the Viking period back to life.
Tel. 76 05 60 00. www. vestvagoy.kommune.no

ℹ Vågan
This island municipality is made up of Austvågøy, part of Hinnøy, and a few smaller islands. The main town of Svolvær is the focus of the islands' local administration, its most important fishing port, a stop on the Hurtigruten line, and, for many visitors, the gateway to the entire Lofoten archipelago. The town is home to a lively art scene, and it's no coincidence that the Nordnorsk Kunstnersentrum (The Art Museum of Northern Norway) is located here. Svolvær is also the starting point of the popular daytrip to the Trollfjord. The Lofoten Museum and the Lofoten Aquarium, containing seals and unusual fish that live in the Arctic Ocean, are both to be found in Kalbvåg, a village on Austvågøy that is thought to date back to the Stone Age.
Svolvær; Tel 75 42 00 00.
www.vagan.kommune.no

Vesterålen

(See p. 144.)

Vesterålsmuseet
Founded in 1920, the Vesterålen Museum is housed in the Melbo Hovedgård mansion, and the decor dates from the turn of the 20th century. The pictures, documents, videos, and many original exhibits really bring the cultural history of the Vesterålen district to life.
Maren Frederiksens allé 1, Melbu; Tel 76 15 75 56; Jun–mid-Aug 11.00–17.00 daily, mid-Aug–May Mon–Fri 9.00–15.00.

Andøy Friluftssenter
The cabins rented out by the Andøy Outdoor company sleep up to eight people. They come with an electric hob and refrigerator, and, thanks to the excellent insulation, are suitable as both winter and summer accommodation. The complex also has its own restaurant, where the food is prepared using locally sourced ingredients.
Buksnesfjord, Risøyhamn; Tel 76 14 88 04. www.andoy-friluftssenter.no

Arctic Sea Kayak Race (ASKR)
This annual kayaking event has been attracting visitors from all over Europe every year since 1991. It's held at the end of July in the fishing village of Skipnes. The participants are a mixed crowd of both beginners and the more experienced, but the overriding emphasis on having fun is common to everyone. Choose from hotel or self-catering camping accommodation. You can hire a kayak on arrival.
Skipnes. www.askr.no

Fjord tour
The *Anna Rogde* went into service in 1868. This double-masted schooner made it possible to transport perishable goods like fruit and vegetables to the North Sea ports, and even as far as the Iberian peninsula. Restored to its former glory in the 1980s, it is now used for pleasure cruises. The ship can carry up to 70 day-trippers, and for longer voyages, its seven cabins sleep up to 20 passengers.
Harstad, Merkurveien 21; Tel 77 00 55 10. www.annarogde.no

Strand Hotell
This family-run hotel in Sortland has everything you'll need for a relaxing break. Staff can also help book excursions and whale-watching trips. In the evenings, the hotel restaurant serves Arctic cuisine, accompanied by bread from the hotel's very own bakery. There are 37 guest rooms, each with its own, distinct character.
Strandgata 34, Sortland; Tel 76 11 00 80. www.strandhotell.no

Senja

(See p. 142)

Ånderdalen National Park
This extensive national park spans 125 sq. km (48 sq. miles) of the southern part of the island of Senja. The park's vast pine and birch forests enjoy protected status, and some rare orchid varieties thrive on its moorlands. Though there are no marked hiking trails, there are good paths. With a bit of luck, you might even get a glimpse of the reindeer and elk that live

in this protected area. You'll find occasional rest huts along the way.
Senja Reiseliv AS, Hamn i Senja; Tel 77 85 98 80. www.hamnisenja.no

Hulder-og Trollparken
Meet the world's largest troll. It lives on the fairytale island of Senja, and – at a height of 18 m (59 feet) – is literally full of surprises. Inside, there's a whole theme park of family-friendly attractions, including an exhibition of paintings by one of the park's owners. Viking helmets, tankards, and soup dishes are amongst the items you can pick up in the souvenir shop.
Finnsæter, Skaland; Tel 77 85 88 64; Jun–Aug 9.00–21.00 daily. www.senjatrollet.no

Tromsø

(See p. 140.)

Ishavskatedralen
The most interesting piece of architecture in Tromsø is surely the Arctic Cathedral. Built in 1965, its walls are made of concrete covered with sheets of aluminum, giving the effect of huge shards of ice. The cathedral is also noted for its 23-m (75-foot) high triangular, stained-glass window, designed by the Norwegian artist Victor Sparre. The window covers an area of 140 sq. m (1,506 sq. feet), and forms the entire eastern wall of the building. It is one of the largest stained-glass windows in Europe.
Hans Nilsens veg 41; Tel 77 75 34 50; Jun–Aug Mon–Sat 9.00–19.00, Sun 13.00–19.00, mid-Aug–mid-Sept 15.00–18.00 daily, mid-Sept–May 16.00–18.00 daily. www.ishavskatedralen.no

Polaria
The Polaria experience combines the aquarium's numerous tanks with attractions such as a panoramic cinema and displays about the polar region. Opened in 1997, two of Polaria's most popular attractions are the films about Spitsbergen and the Antarctic (the former shot from a helicopter flying above the island). The Bearded Seals in the aquarium are another big crowd pleaser, and seal feeding time (12.30 and 15.30 daily) is always entertaining.
Hjalmar Johansens gate 12; Tel 77 75 01 00; Mid-May–mid-Aug 10.00–19.00 daily, mid-Aug–mid-May 12.00–17.00 daily. www.polaria.no

Compagniet
Open only at weekends, Compagniet is one of the city's hottest nightspots. It stands out for its unusual wooden building alone. Dance the night away to the sounds of disco, pop, and rock, as chosen by one of the club's various DJs.
Sjøgata 12; Tel 77 66 42 22; Fri, Sat 22.00–3.30. www.compagniet.no

Vertshuset Skarven
Vertshuset Skarven brings together several restaurants under one roof. Mussels and reindeer soup are the special dishes at Vertshuset, while steaks large and small – and other meat dishes – are the order of the day at Biffhuset. Arctandria, meanwhile, serves a wide range of fish and seafood. Enjoy a cocktail or coffee at the Skarven Bar.
Strandtorget 1; Tel 77 60 07 20. www.skarven.no

An increasingly rare glimpse of nature in all its unspoiled glory (from left): Passing Stor Finnkjerka on a tour of the fjord; the island city of Tromsø; sled dogs in action; and the inside of a Sami hut.

FINNMARK AND TROMS

These pages give additional information for the area described in the "Highlights" chapter (pp. 126–147).

Amalie Hotell
This friendly hotel enjoys a tranquil location close to the water, within easy reach of numerous local restaurants. Its 48 guest rooms come with cable TV and coffee machine, and computers with wireless internet access are also available. The hotel restaurant opens for dinner, but you can make yourself a waffle if you fancy a snack in the afternoon.
Sjøgata 5b; Tel 77 66 48 00.
www.amalie-hotell.no

Kautokeino

Samekniv
Most of the residents of Kautokeino are Sami, so it's no surprise to find shops selling traditional Sami handicrafts. Among them, Samekniv stocks a large range of different types and sizes of knives, as well as wooden boxes, wooden cutlery (mostly made of birch), and leather shoes. Samekniv is the gallery of local Sami knifesmith Josef Per Buljo and a good place to visit if you are looking for gifts to take home.
Galaniittuluodda;
Tel 78 48 62 84;
Mon–Fri 9.00–18.00.
www.samekniv.com

Arctic Motell
This motel also rents out holiday houses with bathrooms and fully equipped kitchens. There's a kiosk, souvenir shop, and children's play area on site, and, in the evening, guests can learn about Sami life and culture from the owner herself. In winter, the motel is open to pre-booked parties only. Worth a visit to find out more about the fascinating Sami culture.
Suomaluodda 16;
Tel 78 48 54 00.
www.kauto.no

Karasjok

Sápmi
The Sápmi theme park is a fun way to discover the history, culture, and customs of the Sami. Audiences at the Stálubákti ("the magical theater") are taken on a journey into the depths of Sami mythology, while the summer and winter dwellings provide a hands-on insight into the day-to-day life of a Sami family – a way of life in which reindeer husbandry is often an important component. Visitors can also try some typical Sami dishes, and buy Sami crafts.
Tel 78 36 88 10.

Storgammen
This restaurant belongs to the Rica Hotel, and the unforgettable culinary experience of dining here is steeped in local tradition. The menu – which includes reindeer stew and smoked reindeer hearts – is all based on age-old Sami recipes. The restaurant itself is housed in a wood and peat hut, and diners enjoy their food sitting on reindeer furs around the dining room's open fire.
Leavnnjageaidnu 1;
Tel 78 46 88 60.
www.ricahotels.com/Hotels/Rica-Hotel-Karasjok

Alta
(See p. 138.)

Alta Kommune
Though an important commercial area, Alta is best known for the nearby rock paintings, which date back between 2,500 and 6,000 years. The drawings are designated a UNESCO World Heritage Site, and there is an educational trail to guide you through their depictions of hunting and dancing scenes, and their geometric shapes and symbols. Alternatively, the Alta Museum documents the region's local history. In March, the world's longest dog sled race takes place here, and the Sautso canyon – south-east of Alta – is also impressive.
Sandfallveien 1;
Tel 78 45 50 00.
www.alta.kommune.no

Kirkenes
(See p. 134.)

Tourist information
The port of Kirkenes is the last and most northerly stop on the Hurtigruten line. It's only a short distance from here to the Russian border, and the Russian market is one of the town's main attractions. The area's cross-border heritage is shown in more detail at the Grenseland Museum. The Savio Museum, meanwhile, is home to an extensive collection of paintings and woodcarvings by Sami artists.
Kirkenes Touristinformasjon, Presteveien 1; Tel 78 99 25 44.
www.kirkenesinfo.no

Hammerfest

Isbjørnklubben
Run by Hammerfest's Polar Bear Society, the small museum in the town hall explores the area's Arctic history. There's a particular emphasis on hunting and fishing, and an almost 3-m (10-foot) long polar bear fur is one of the most prized exhibits.
Tel 78 41 31 00;
Mid-Jun–mid-Aug Mon–Fri 6.00–16.00, Sat, Sun 6.00–15.00, mid-Aug–mid-Jun Mon–Fri 10.00–14.00, Sat, Sun 10.30–13.30.
www.isbjornklubben.no

Hotell Skytterhuset
Free internet access, a sauna, and cable TV are just some of the amenities at the Hotell Skytterhuset. There are 75 nicely furnished guest rooms and a well-developed garden – perfect if it's a bit of peace and quiet you're looking for. Good value for money.
Skytterveien 24;
Tel 78 42 20 10.
www.skytterhuset.no

Vardø

Vardø Kommune
This island municipality is connected to the mainland by an 800-m (2,625-foot) long undersea tunnel. At its deepest point, the tunnel is some 88 m (289 feet) below sea level. Don't miss Vardøhus Festning (Fortress) – built in the shape of an eight-pointed star, its origins go all the way back to the 14th century. Polar expeditions are amongst the topics explored at the Vardø Museum.
Tel. 78 94 33 00.
www.vardo.kommune.no

The North Cape
(See p. 130.)

Nordkapp Kommune
On a clear day, the view from the North Cape – on the northern coast of the island of Magerøya – is simply stunning. If the weather's less amenable, get the best view you can from the North Cape Hall's panoramic restaurant. A path from the North Cape leads to the headland of Knivskjelodden, the northernmost point in Europe.
Honningsvåg;
Tel 78 47 65 00.
www.nordkapp.no

Spitsbergen

(See p. 154.)

🏛 Atelier Aino

Paintings, drawings, prints, and posters by Aino Grib are all on show in this local artist's own gallery. Grib's polar surroundings are the inspiration behind his work, and the area's landscape, wildlife, and Northern Lights are his subjects.
Longyearbyen;
Tel 79 02 10 02.
www.ainogrib.com

🏛 Gallery Svalbard

The collection includes works by a whole range of Norwegian painters, most of whom have found inspiration in Spitsbergen. The gallery also houses a map collection, bookshop, and craft workshops – all of which provide a suitably inspiring setting for the occasional music concerts held here.
Longyearbyen;
Tel 79 02 15 57.

🏛 Spitsbergen Airship Museum

Opened at the end of 2008, the museum explores the importance of airships in man's conquest of the Arctic. The display is in fact devoted to three specific airships, namely the America, Norge, and Italia. It was on board the America that Walter Wellman twice attempted to fly over the North Pole. Both attempts – the first in 1907, the second in 1909 – were unsuccessful, and it was 1926 before Roald Amundsen, Lincoln Ellsworth, and Umberto Nobile finally overflew the Pole in the Norge. Nobile's flights in the Italia, meanwhile, yielded important scientific data

about the Arctic. Model aircraft, documents, pictures, and stamps are just some of the many interesting exhibits.
Tel 79 02 17 05;
10.00–18.00 daily.
www.spitsbergenairshipmuseum.com

🏛 Svalbard Kirke

Alongside regular services and church occasions, Svalbard Church also hosts concerts, readings, and other cultural events. Both visitors and Longyearbyen residents are welcome at the church's occasional coffee and cake afternoons.
Longyearbyen;
Tel 79 02 55 60.
www.svalbardkirke.no

🏛 Svalbard Museum

Opened in 1979, the Svalbard Museum moved to its current home within the Svalbard Science Center in 2005. It is devoted to both Svalbard's natural environment, and the culture and customs of its inhabitants. Two of the most interesting parts of the museum are the seawater aquarium and the reconstruction of an 18th-century whaling station. The importance of mining on the archipelago also comes under the spotlight, and a further section traces the polar expeditions of Norwegian explorers like Fridtjof Nansen and Roald Amundsen.
Longyearbyen;
Tel 79 02 64 92;
May–Sept 10.00–17.00 daily,
Oct–Apr 12.00–17.00 daily.
www.svalbardmuseum.no

🔍 Cave walk

Discover the magical world of the glaciers on a guided tour of a glacial cave. You'll see a

landscape of glistening ice crystals, deep ice columns, and gigantic ice blocks. Helmets and head torches are provided by the tour organizer.
Svalbard Wildlife Expeditions AS;
Tel 79 02 22 22;
Mon, Tues, Thurs, Sun 10.00–13.00, Wed, Fri 16.00–19.00.
www.wildlife.no

🔍 Dog sled trips

The best way to reach the remotest parts of the Arctic is by dog sled. These trips are a chance to discover the breadth and majesty of the Spitsbergen landscape, while also learning how to drive a dog sled and work with the animals effectively. Trips last from one to several days, and you can hire the necessary specialist clothing and equipment (including wind and waterproof jackets and trousers, boots, and sleeping bags) before departure.
Spitsbergen Travel.
www.spitsbergentravel.no

🔍 Ingeniør G. Paulsen AS

If you'd prefer to explore independently, this is the place to hire both a snowmobile and the specialist clothing and other equipment you'll need to go with it. Rifles are also available – if you're journeying deep inland, you might need one to defend yourself against polar bear attack.
Longyearbyen;
Tel 79 02 32 00; Feb–mid-May Mon–Fri 9.00–17.00, Sat 11.00–14.00;
mid-May–Jan Mon–Fri 10.00–16.30, Sat 12.00–14.00.
www.spitsbergentravel.no/igp

🔍 Kjell Henriksen Observatory

The observatory is set over some 700 sq. km (270 sq. miles). It's charged with researching the middle and upper atmosphere, and various optical instruments and other pieces of equipment are used to this end. Call in advance to arrange a guided tour of the grounds. Paintings by Norwegian artist Marius Martinussen adorn some of the observatory corridors.
Breinosa;
Tel 98 28 51 74.
http://kho.unis.no

🔍 Boat trips

A trip along the Spitsbergen coast in a ship like the MS Norstjernen or MS Expedition is an unforgettable experience. The ships sail close to the coastline, passing calving glaciers and awe-inspiring mountains. It's also an excellent way to discover Spitsbergen's plant and animal life.
Spitsbergen Travel,
Longyearbyen;
Tel 79 02 61 00.
www.spitsbergentravel.no

🔍 Snowmobiling

These snowmobile trips start in Longyearbyen and last several hours. They head off in all different directions, some going right across the island to the glaciers and fjords. It's especially exciting during the polar winter. Participants will need a valid driving licence (car or motorcycle). The chances of seeing the Northern Lights are particularly good during the dark season.
Svalbard Snøscooterutleie,
Longyearbyen;
Tel 79 02 46 61.
www.svalbard.net/scooterutleie

Cold and distant (from left): The Smeerenburg glacier on Spitsbergen; Beerenberg volcano on the remote island of Jan Mayen; the Huset restaurant; and inside the Spitsbergen Hotel.

SPITSBERGEN

These pages give additional information for the area described in the "Highlights" chapter (pp. 148–157).

Spitsbergen marathon
The Spitsbergen marathon, which takes place every June, is a Longyearbyen tradition. The 42-km (26-mile) course starts and ends at the Svalbardhallen sports complex, and there's also a 21-km (13-mile) half marathon race. It attracts lots of international runners.
Longyearbyen;
Tel 79 02 13 33.
www.svalbardturn.no

Svalbard ski marathon
The ski marathon takes place in April. The 42-km (26-mile) course starts and ends in Adventdalen, passing through some fantastic countryside. It's open to anyone who thinks they are up to the challenge, and there's also a 21-km (13-mile) half marathon option. The prize-giving ceremony and victory celebrations take place in Longyearbyen's Svalbardhallen in the evening.
Adventdalen;
Tel 79 02 13 33.
www.svalbardturn.no

Gollgruva Arctic Design AS
This shop stocks textiles, outdoor equipment, and craft pieces. There's winter clothing, kit for all sorts of outdoor activities, and some elegant gold and silver jewelry items, including bracelets, chains, and rings.
Longyearbyen;
Tel 79 02 18 16.

RaBi's Bua
If it's embroidery, woollen clothing (especially for women and children), curtains, carpets, and home accessories you're after, you'll find them all here. Many of the textiles are decorated

with cheerful, Arctic motifs.
Longyearbyen;
Tel 79 02 10 48.
www.rabisbua.no

Svalbardbutikken
A visit to Longyearbyen's biggest shopping complex is a chance to pick up souvenirs, electronics, perfumes, alcoholic drinks, tobacco, chocolate, and more. There's also a wide range of foodstuffs, including fresh fruit and vegetables.
Longyearbyen;
Tel 79 02 25 25;
Mon–Fri 10.00–20.00,
Sat 10.00–18.00, Sun
15.00–18.00.

Arctic Pub Invest
With a range of alcoholic and non-alcoholic drinks you'll struggle to find anywhere else like it in Norway; it's not just the exceptionally cozy atmosphere that makes this bar such a popular meeting place. If you don't want to stop, you can also buy drink to take with you.
Longyearbyen;
Tel 79 02 25 11.

Huset
This local eatery combines the feel of a restaurant with that of a coffee house. Arctic dishes on the menu include game, reindeer, and fish – all of which will go nicely with one of the 20,000-odd bottles of wine in the cellar. The restaurant's adjoining nightclub is one of Spitsbergen nightlife's few hotspots.
Longyearbyen;
Tel 79 02 25 03;
restaurant Sun–Fri
16.00–23.00,
Sat 14.00–23.00,
nightclub Fri
Sat 23.00–4.00.
www.huset.com

Radisson SAS Polar Hotel Spitsbergen
Completed in 1995, the hotel has 95 rooms in a range of sizes (42 standard rooms, 25 superior rooms, and 28 apartments). The first floor superior rooms enjoy a superb view of the Isfjord and surrounding area, while the apartments, which each sleep up to five people, are located in a separate block next door. Diners at the hotel restaurant (11.00–18.00 daily) are treated to a menu of Arctic dishes. The Barentz Pub & Spiseri, meanwhile, is one of the most popular meeting places on the entire island (Mon, Tues 16.00–1.00, Wed–Sun 16.00–2.00).
Longyearbyen;
Tel 79 02 34 50.
www.longyearbyen.radisson
sas.com

Spitsbergen Guesthouse
The 75 guest rooms at the Spitsbergen Guesthouse are split between three buildings. The converted living quarters offer a total of 124 beds in single, double and triple rooms. Each building has its own breakfast room, as well as a kitchen in which guests can prepare their own food. In the afternoon you can make fresh waffles to go with your coffee or tea. There's also a laundry room and communal computer with internet access in all three buildings, as well as numerous bathrooms with toilets and showers. Excursions including glacier hikes and dog sled racing can be booked at reception. It all represents very good value for money.
Longyearbyen;
Tel 79 02 63 00.

Spitsbergen Hotel
This well-designed building was once used as accommodation for employees of a local mining company. Now a hotel, it has 88 guest rooms. The Funktionærmessen Restaurant serves French-inspired dishes complemented by an excellent choice of fine wines, and in the afternoon there are freshly made waffles on offer in the lounge. There's also a well-equipped spa area, complete with sauna and massage benches.
Longyearbyen;
Tel 79 02 62 00.
http://www.rica.se/en/Hotels/
Spitsbergen-Hotel/

Jan Mayen
(See p. 156.)

Climbing Beerenberg
At a height of 2,277 m (7,470 feet), the Beerenberg volcano is the highest point on the entire 373-sq. km (144-sq. mile) island. It can be climbed as part of a prebooked tour, although frequently atrocious weather conditions mean that expeditions in this mountainous region are limited to just a few days a year. The volcano last erupted in the mid-1980s. The eruption lasted two days. A red glow lit the sky and a plume of smoke rose above the volcano as lava flowed down to the sea. It is generally considered to be the most northerly volcano in the world. It is composed primarily of basaltic lava flows with minor amounts of tephra. It is believed to have erupted in 1732 and 1818.
Tel. 32 17 79 00,
www.jan-mayen.no

NORWAY EXPLORER

MAJOR CITIES

Many of Norway's large cities are found along the Norwegian Sea coastline, and frequently at the mouths of the fjords, which stretch deep into the country's interior. Their ports and waterfronts have been well restored, and some older districts have managed to retain their medieval charm, despite their modern infrastructure. Their narrow alleyways are lined with wooden houses that are often brightly decorated. A range of museums documents the history of shipbuilding, seafaring, fishing, and oil extraction – fields in which this Scandinavian country has traditionally been a world leader. Last but not least, Norway's visual arts scene is inspired by a wide variety of themes and styles.

Sights

❶ Slottet

The Royal Palace sits atop a hill, surrounded by a vast park that is open to the public. This elongated building, designed in the Empire style and comprising three wings, was built between 1825 and 1848 under the direction of King Karl Johan of Sweden and Norway (although he did not live to see its completion), but it only became the king's permanent residence following the 1905 declaration of Norwegian independence. The palace houses an art collection, and a statue of King Karl Johan on horseback stands in front of the main building.

❷ Historisk Museum

The Historical Museum brings together three valuable collections – the Antiquities Collection, the Ethnographic Museum, and the Collection of Coins and Medals – which together document Norway's history from the first Neolithic settlements right up to the present day. The Viking era enjoys particular prominence, as does religious art from the Middle Ages, in an exhibition boasting various relics from the stave churches. The collection devoted to Inuit culture is also unique.

❸ The National Gallery

The National Gallery (Nasjonalgalleriet) is Norway's largest collection of paintings, sculptures, and engravings, containing a spectacular array of works by artists such as the great Norwegian painter Edvard Munch (whose The Scream is housed in the gallery). One entire section is devoted to the French Impressionists including Cézanne and Manet, and another exhibits paintings by artists such as El Greco, Rubens, and Rembrandt.

❹ Rådhuset

The immense City Hall building (constructed between 1931 and 1950) is one of Oslo's landmarks, with a somewhat bare brick facade that hides a grandly designed interior, richly decorated with frescoes. The City Hall is the venue for the Nobel Peace Prize Award Ceremony, which takes place every year on 10 December. (See p. 60.)

❺ Stortinget

The neo-Gothic parliament building, built between 1861 and 1866, resembles an ancient amphitheater. The hall's showpiece is an Oscar Wergeland painting, depicting the assembly that ratified the Norwegian constitution in 1814.

❻ Oslo Cathedral

The city's cathedral was consecrated in 1697, and its altar and pulpit date back to that era. There have been various 20th-century additions to the design of the cathedral, including Emmanuel Vigeland's glass paintings, as well as ceiling paintings by Hugo Louis Mohr.

❼ Museet for samtidskunst

The Museum of Contemporary Art holds the most comprehensive collection of post-1945 modern art to be found in Norway, and displays paintings, sculptures, installations, and photographs from local artists. The museum building, once a bank, also houses a popular collection of international contemporary art.

❽ Akershus Fortress

The end of the 13th century saw the construction of a fortress above the Oslofjord, and this structure withstood repeated enemy onslaughts until its 17th-century transformation into a renaissance castle. Various Norwegian kings are buried in the castle mausoleum. Today, the castle is used as a venue for welcoming important state guests.

❾ Aker Brygge

In 1982, the Akers Mekaniske Verksted shipyard closed its doors, having built more than 500 ships. The renovated shipyard building is now home to various restaurants and boutiques, and sits in harmony with the modern glass and steel buildings (as well as the marina) that have sprung up near by – an example of successful redevelopment.

❿ Bygdøy

The Bygdøy peninsula is the location for some of Oslo's most interesting museums. The Norsk Sjøfartsmuseum is a maritime museum documenting the important local traditions of seafaring, shipbuilding, and fishing. The Fram Museum boasts possession of Fridtjof Nansen's polar ship Fram, the Kon-Tiki Museum houses Thor Heyerdahl's legendary raft, the Vikingskiphuset contains some Viking ships, and the Norsk Folkemuseum is the largest open-air museum in Europe. (See p. 64.)

⓫ Vigelandsparken

This area of the Frogner Park is named after Gustav Vigeland. It contains many of his sculptures, including the Monolith composed of 121 human figures.

Eating and drinking

❶ Statholdergaarden

Bent Stiansen, the Oslo-based winner of the Bocuse d'Or, has transformed this restaurant into one of the finest in Norway. It offers a six-course menu that is tailored to the season, and the cellars contain many a fine wine.
Rådhusgata 11;
Tel 22 41 88 00;
Mon–Sat 18.00–24.00.
www.statholdergaarden.no

From left: The Gokstad ship in the Vikingskipshuset; Oslo's main landmark is the City Hall; the 17th-century Domkirke is the largest cathedral in the city; in the Statholdergaarden.

OSLO

Located at the end of the Oslofjord, the Norwegian capital city is the king's primary residence and the seat of government; it also has a university and many world-famous museums. The city's architecture successfully combines the traditional and modern.

② Lofoten Fiskerestaurant
The decor of this elegant fish and seafood restaurant follows a maritime theme. Signature dishes include scallops and red king crabs, and the view from the terrace over the Oslofjord is beyond compare. A feast for the eye and the palate.
Stranden 75; Tel 22 83 08 08; Mon–Sat 11.00–1.00, Sun 12.00–24.00. www. lofoten-fiskerestaurant.no

③ Theatercafeen
Artists, bankers, and tourists alike come to the Theatercafeen to enjoy and relax in its lively atmosphere and to try the excellent selection of dishes and snacks. You could also come for nothing more than a nice cup of coffee and to enjoy the ambience. The menu includes a variety of Norwegian fare, as well as dishes from other European countries.
Stortingsgata 24/26;

Tel 22 82 40 00; Mon–Sat 11.00–23.00, Sun 15.00–22.00. www.theatercafeen.no

④ Kaffistova
The Kaffistova restaurant in the Hotel Bondeheimen specializes in Norwegian cuisine, serving a variety of local dishes including *boknafisk* (dried, salted fish), whale steak, and *rømmegrøt* (sour cream porridge), as well as a traditional Norwegian breakfast.

A selection of homemade cakes is offered for dessert.
Rosenkrantzgate 8; Tel 23 21 42 10; Mon–Fri 10.00–20.00, Sat, Sun 10.00–17.00. www.bondeheimen.no

Accommodation

⑤ Hotel Bristol
The Bristol is considered one of the capital city's best addresses, boasting 251 spacious and comfortably furnished rooms. The hotel contains a restaurant, offering both Norwegian and international cuisine, as well as a cozy bar. Other amenities include a gym and a sauna.
Kristian IV's gate 7; Tel 22 82 60 00. www.bristol.no

⑥ Thon Hotel Opera
This four-star hotel near Oslo's main station offers 434 rooms of various types – from perfectly furnished suites to well-equipped singles. Most rooms offer a view of either the main part of the city or the Oslofjord. A gym and spa are also available.
Christian Frederiks plass 5; Tel 24 10 30 00. www.thonhotels.com/opera

Shopping

⑦ Norway Design
Located directly opposite the Nationaltheatret, this shopping precinct sells crafts and accessories, offering a range of goods from glassware and ceramics, to clothing and hardware.
Stortingsgata 28; Tel 23 11 45 10; Mon–Fri 9.00–17.00 (Sun until 19.00), Sat 10.00–15.00. www.norwaydesign.no

Sights

❶ Norsk Hermetikkmuseum

The Norwegian Canning Museum is housed in a former canning factory (which dates from 1873) and offers visitors an insight into the process of how fish is packed into tins, an industry which was once as important for Stavanger as the business of crude oil is today. The last sardines were processed here in the 1950s. The museum also houses a weird and wonderful collection of can labels (see p. 21).

❷ Gamle Stavanger

The old town district of Gamle Stavanger stretches west from Vågen bay. Its landscape is characterized by some 160 18th-century wooden houses, as well as their narrow, cobbled alleyways first built during the 19th century. The whitewashed wooden houses, all equipped with gardens and located between the residential streets of Øvre Strandgate and Nedre Strandgate, are particularly beautiful. Some of the buildings are protected sites of historic interest, and the inhabitants have successfully resisted all efforts to modernize or commercialize the district. (See p. 20.)

❸ Stavanger Sjøfartsmuseum

This maritime museum, lying directly on the seafront, contains ships dating from a variety of eras, and documents the history of seafaring and port life in Norway. One of the most prominent examples is the *Wyvern*, built in around 1897, and the *Anna af Sand*, which was launched in 1848.

The latter, the oldest Norwegian sailing ship still in use, is moored here when not at sea.

❹ Valbergtårnet

This watchtower, completed in 1853, can be found on Valberget hill. At first, it was used by the fire services as a lookout point, but this did not prevent Stavanger from being repeatedly devastated by large fires. Valbergtårnet offers a fantastic view of the main city, as well as of the comings and goings in the port. The Vektermuseet (Watchman's Museum) in the higher levels of this historic building attracts many visitors wanting to understand more about the Valbergtårnet and its history.

❺ Norsk Oljemuseum

Since the 1960s, Stavanger has profited considerably from the extraction of crude oil in the North Sea. The architecturally impressive, ultramodern oil museum, opened in 1999, contains an informative exhibition detailing how this raw material is transformed into the "black gold" that is so important for the city. Items on display include drill bits and diving bells, and a reconstructed oil rig allows visitors to try their hand at operating a drill.

❻ St Svithuns Cathedral

This cathedral on the tiny lake of Breiavatnet is one of the most significant medieval church buildings in Norway. The Romanesque cathedral, completed in 1125, is named after St Svithun, the patron saint of Stavanger. It was badly damaged during a fire in 1272 and rebuilt in a predominantly Gothic style, but the grand interior is primarily

baroque. The towers on the eastern side, topped off by pyramid-shaped roofs, were added in the middle of the 18th century, and the stained-glass window depicting New Testament scenes was fitted in 1957. (See p. 20.)

❼ Stavanger Museum

This museum, whose primary building was completed at the end of the 19th century, is split into a variety of interesting sections, including a zoological collection containing a multitude of birds from Scandinavia and other regions. The museum actively conducts research into animal habits, and publicizes its recent findings. The Maritime Museum specializes in the maritime history of southwestern Norway and has collections of artifacts, archives, and photographs. The Canning Museum is located in a former canning factory and explains the complete canning process.

❽ Arkeologisk Museum

The Museum of Archeology illustrates the history of the region, with the help of various cultural and historical relics. Settlement remains, ship timbers, cultural items, equipment, weapons, musical instruments, and much more all create an evocative portrait of daily life since the Stone Age.

❾ Ledaal

For many years, this estate (built in 1799 in the Empire style) belonged to a prosperous family. Today, it is the royal family's Stavanger residence. When the royals are not staying in Ledaal, tourists can visit the building and its small, but interesting, museum.

Eating and drinking

❶ Jans mat- og vinhus

Stavanger's most expensive restaurant deserves its reputation as the city's best, having won a plethora of prizes. Its imaginatively prepared fare includes a number of fish dishes, and the ambience is equally enjoyable. The predominantly Norwegian menu is very refined with flourishes of French cuisine. This is a top class restaurant that will satisfy (almost) every food lover. Gourmets will love it here.
Breitorget 6–8, near Breitgata; Tel 51 55 11 11; Tues–Sat 19.00–24.00. www.jans.no

❷ Harry Pepper

Harry Pepper is unusual, but perhaps offers some light relief: this Mexican restaurant was the first of its kind in Norway when it opened its doors in 1986. The Tex-Mex offerings are more than a little spicy, with the chili con carne and the lamb in mustard sauce being the most popular. After dinner, the Tequila Saloon beckons diners in to enjoy a variety of cocktails.
Øvre Holmegate 15; Tel 51 89 39 59; Mon 18.00–24.00, Tues–Sat 18.00–1.00. www.harry-pepper.no

❸ Bistrohuset

Restaurant, bistro, café, or bar? Bistrohuset brings various eateries together under one roof, including the City Brasserie & Vinbar as well as the City Bistro restaurant.
Madlaveien 18; Tel 51 53 95 70; Mon 18.00–24.00, Tues–Sat 18.00–1.00. www.bistrohuset.no

STAVANGER

This city first earned fame for processing fish, and then later for the extraction of crude oil, with the latter having a major impact on Stavanger's economic growth. However, the city has retained its charm, and its inhabitants are cosmopolitan and open-minded.

❹ Straen Fiskerestaurant

This is one of the best fish restaurants in Stavanger. Its 1950s decor is genuine and adds to the cozy atmosphere, and every meal here includes a fantastic view of the port thrown in for free.
Nedre Strandgate 15;
Tel 51 84 37 00;
Mon–Sat 18.00–1.30.
www.herlige-restauranter.no/
straenfiskerestaurant

Accommodation

❺ Skagen Brygge Hotell

This hotel has a magnificent location. After a stroll round the city, guests can return in the evening to relax and refresh in the Turkish baths, or make use of the sauna and gym facilities. The restaurant and bar have been reviewed in the international press, and the hotel offers attractive rates for weekend breaks.
Skagenkaien 30;
Tel 51 85 00 00.
www.skagenbryggehotell.no

❻ Rogalandsheimen Inn

This is one of the oldest and most comfortable lodgings in the city. Its 15 rooms differ in size and can accommodate up to five people. There are various communal areas.
Musegata 18; Tel 51 52 01 88.
www.rogalandsheimen.no

Shopping

❼ Oleana

The popular designer Solveig Hisdal has created a range of stylish clothing and accessories – including jackets, sweaters, wristbands, scarves, and hats.
Kirkegata 31;
Tel 51 89 48 04.
www.oleana.no

Sights

❶ Norges fiskerimuseum
Visitors to the Norwegian Fisheries Museum (situated near the ferry port) are granted a comprehensive overview of how the catching, processing, and sale of fish have developed over the years. The museum also documents the history of fish farming, sealing, and whaling in the area.

❷ Bergenhus festning
This 12th-century fortress is home to Haakon's Hall, named after King Haakon Haakonson. This ceremonial hall, the largest secular building to be constructed in medieval Norway, is now used to host state receptions, concerts, and various other festivities.

❸ Mariakirken
The oldest sections of St Mary's Church, constructed in a mix of Romanesque and Gothic styles, date from the 12th century – making this the oldest church in Bergen. It is opulently designed and fantastically flamboyant, at least by Protestant standards. The magnificent 17th-century pulpit is adorned with images of the Christian virtues.

❹ Bryggens Museum
This museum offers an insight into daily life in a medieval city, with exhibits including archeological finds (such as the remains of 12th-century buildings), parts of ships, rune inscriptions, and paintings.

❺ Bryggen
Each of the 121 spacious rooms (including 21 suites) are decorated with works of art. The warehouses also hark back to the heyday of the Hanseatic

League. They suffered damage in a series of fires but were carefully restored. The district is now also home to artists. (See p. 34.)

❻ Hanseatic Museum
The Hanseatic Museum, opened in 1872, can be found in one of the Hanseatic houses that belonged to former times to German merchants. Exhibits of tools, seals, and the equipment used for drying fish – when Bergen was one of the most important ports in the Hanseatic League – brings the Late Middle Ages to life. (See p. 35.)

❼ Bergen Cathedral
Bergen's Romanesque cathedral was built in the middle of the 13th century, and its 60-m (200-foot) long Gothic chancel was completed in 1537. The impressive altar resembles a medieval reliquary casket, and the Gothic windows are especially beautiful.

❽ Grieghallen
The Grieghallen complex is used as a venue for a variety of opera and drama performances, not least the Bergen International Festival. The 1,500-seat concert hall, opened in 1978, is the largest auditorium of its kind in Norway, and a second hall seats 600. The city's Filharmoniske Orkester regularly gives performances in the Grieghallen.

❾ The Natural History Collections in Bergen Museum
This fascinating museum of natural history includes areas devoted to geology, zoology, and botany and the scientific collections are varied. They include specimens from

research projects and private gifts. Some of its greatest attractions include a reconstructed whale skeleton, a botanical garden, and greenhouses full of tropical plants that bloom in every shade imaginable.

❿ The Cultural History Collections in Bergen Museum
This collection of cultural and historical items focuses particularly on Norwegian life and tradition. Objects are arranged by period – for example, the Stone Age or the Viking era – and the collection also highlights other cultures from around the world. The museum additionally houses a collection of religious art, including a selection of Russian icons.

⓫ Sjøfartsmuseum
Opened in 1921, this museum is dedicated to Norwegian maritime history from the Viking ships right up to the most modern vessels, paying particular attention to the harsh conditions of life at sea. Children can join in by sending remote-controlled model ships off on (reasonably) long journeys of their own. It's a great place to visit with little ones.

⓬ Den Nationale Scene
The National Venue of Theater, housed in an imposing art nouveau building, is one of Bergen's landmarks. This stage, rich in tradition, first came into being as the Norsk Theater (established in 1850), where the great Norwegian dramatist Henrik Ibsen worked as manager for six years from 1851. The playhouse's ambitious choice of repertoire has gained it a reputation as world class.

Eating and drinking

❶ Holbergstuen
This restaurant, opened in 1927, is as rich in tradition as any in Bergen. Bright and vivid rose painting adds to the atmosphere of nostalgia. Holbergstuen offers a range of traditional Norwegian cuisine, as well as a selection of reasonably priced smaller dishes such as Holberg-burgers. The restaurant is regularly frequented by many of Bergen's artists.
Torgallmenningen 6;
Tel 55 55 20 55;
Mon–Sat 11.00–00.30,
Sun 14.00–23.30.
www.holbergstuen.no

❷ Fiskekrogen Fisk & Vilt Restaurant
This restaurant is one of the best in Bergen and has been awarded numerous prizes. The ingredients arrive fresh from the fish market, and are transformed into refined gourmet dishes. Delicacies such as seafood platters or pan-fried trout are particularly popular with locals and tourists alike.
Torget 2; Tel. 55 55 96 55;
11.00–00.30 daily.

❸ Wesselstuen
The menu in this cozy eatery offers a mix of Norwegian dishes and international cuisine (such as French onion soup), with signature dishes including reindeer fillet with celery purée and red onion, and mussels in saffron and white wine. Wesselstuen also offers a range of tasty sandwiches to satisfy those little hunger pangs.
Ole Bulls plass 6;
Tel 55 55 49 49;
Mon–Sat 11.00–00.30,
Sun 14.00–23.30.
www.wesselstuen.no

From left: Historic warehouses in the port; the Hanseatic Museum near the fish market; a view of the port and the cathedral tower; Neptun Hotel's reception area.

BERGEN

Bergen is one of the most historic cities in Norway. The old wooden houses along the waterfront are a reminder of the city's long commercial tradition. During the Hanseatic era it was a hub for northern trade.

4 Enhjørningen
This fish restaurant in the old Bryggen dockyard offers a wide range of dishes: fish platters, oysters, salmon, halibut, clam chowder, and whale steak are all on offer. Reservations are recommended.
Bryggen 29; Tel 55 32 79 19; 16.00–23.00 daily. www.enhjorningen.no

Accommodation

5 Neptun Hotel
The communal areas of this hotel, as well as each of the 124 spacious rooms (including 21 suites), are adorned with countless artworks. The hotel restaurant has French inspired cuisine and a large and varied wine list.
Valkensdorfgaten 8; Tel 55 30 68 00. www.neptunhotel.no

6 First Marin
The Marin, comprising 152 beautifully furnished rooms, is luxuriously decorated in a variety of styles, with a selection of maritime ornaments on display. The hotel also contains a Jacuzzi and a steam bath for use by its guests.
Rosenkrantzgaten 8; Tel 53 05 15 00. www.firsthotels.com/marin

Shopping

7 Fish market
The fish market, held in the marketplace, is a must for any visitor to Bergen. As well as selling fish straight from the boats, the market also offers fruit and vegetables, flowers, souvenirs, and crafts.
Torget; Tel 55 31 56 17; June–Aug 7.00–17.00 daily, Sept–May Mon–Sat 7.00–16.00.

Sights

❶ Erkebispegården

The Archbishop's Palace, built during the 12th century, was for a long time the political and spiritual heart of the country. Following the Reformation, the property became a private residence for feudal lords, and from the middle of the 17th century it was used as a military base. The buildings house a variety of museums, including the former coin factory and the armoury (Rustkammeret), which contains a collection of firearms. One section focuses on the Norwegian resistance movement which operated during the Nazi occupation between 1940 and 1945.

❷ Nidaros Cathedral

Work began on this cathedral (one of Scandinavia's most impressive church buildings) in the 12th century, building on the site of Olav the Holy's tomb. Reaching 102 m (335 feet) long and around 50 m (160 feet) wide, it is also Norway's largest medieval structure. The sculptures along the facade depict Norwegian saints and biblical figures, and the stained glass designs are singularly superb. The cathedral houses the king's insignia, which is on display for visitors. (See p. 98.)

❸ Kunstindustrimuseum

The National Museum of Decorative Arts has a variety of displays, including old furniture, tapestries, and fixtures, as well as Scandinavian art, chinaware, glass, ceramics, costumes, and an art nouveau collection. One of the museum's most popular areas is its exhibition of Japanese art.

❹ Kunstmuseum

Trondheim Art Museum contains an array of important works by Norwegian painters, the majority of which date from the 19th and 20th centuries, with modern works being particularly prized. A further attraction is the substantial collection of international graphic art.

❺ Vår Frue kirke

Built in the 12th century, the Church of Our Lady has seen a huge amount of change since its beginnings. Much of the architecture was added during extensions and restorations in later years, and the imposing square tower was only finally completed in 1739. The altarpiece was originally in Nidaros Cathedral. The church's interior repeatedly suffered damage from various large fires, but was each time painstakingly restored. The church is less spectacularly striking than the city's cathedral, but its beautifully harmonious layout makes it nonetheless worth a visit.

❻ Vitenskapsmuseet

Trondheim's Museum of Natural History and Archeology, spread over a number of buildings, holds collections owned by the university. The most interesting are the natural history areas, divided into sections focusing on mineralogy, botany, and zoology, as well as the archeological holdings. The library also housed in the museum, containing manuscripts and a permanent exhibition of religious art, is well worth a visit. A further area is devoted to the history of Trondheim since the Viking era.

❼ Stiftsgården

This stately home was constructed in 1770 as a private rococo palace for a wealthy widow wanting to impress the "high society" of Trondheim. The villa, painted a vivid yellow, is one of the most imposing examples of Norwegian wooden architecture and one of the best preserved wooden buildings in the whole of Scandinavia. This building, barely 60 m (200 feet) long, is now the king's regular residence when he is in Trondheim, and at other times is open to visitors; the dining hall, containing a large number of valuable paintings, is particularly impressive (see p. 96).

❽ Sjøfartsmuseet

Trondheim Maritime Museum, housed in a building dating from 1725, contains a wide selection of objects: model ships, figureheads, nautical equipment, and various other maritime relics are on display, some of which were found aboard the frigate Perlen, which sank in 1781.

❾ Kristiansten festning

Visitors to the Kristiansten fortress (which always displays the Norwegian flag) are rewarded with wonderful views of Trondheim and its port, which is particularly beautiful at sunset. The fortress was built in the baroque style at the end of the 17th century, after parts of the city were destroyed by a huge fire in 1681. Encircled by tall, sturdy defensive walls, the fortress has never been captured. The octagonal defensive tower now houses a museum. (See p. 97.)

Eating and drinking

❶ Krambua

A popular restaurant serving fish dishes and a variety of snacks, as well as a tempting selection of homemade desserts. The pub attached to the restaurant is open until midnight (Tues–Sat until 2.00).
Krambugata 12;
Tel 73 53 52 53;
Mon–Sat 11.30–22.00,
Sun 15.00–20.00.
www.krambuatrondheim.no

From left: The wooden Gamle Bybro, the Archbishop's Palace and Nidaros Cathedral; the Kristiansten fortress; Palmehaven restaurant in the Hotel Britannia.

TRONDHEIM

Norway's third largest city has also acted as the country's capital (and royal residence) on occasion. Following the huge fire of 1681, a series of broad boulevards were constructed, in contrast to the angular alleyways lined with wooden houses.

❷ Emilies Et Spisested
Norwegian dishes with echoes of French and Italian. Each five-course menu is individually put together, and guests can also choose from a selection of tapas. The wine list includes offerings from France, Italy, Germany, and South Africa.
Erling Skakkesgate 45;
Tel 73 92 96 41;
Tues–Fri 16.00–23.00,
Sat 18.00–23.00.
www.restaurantakropolis.no

**❸ Havfruen
Fiskerestaurant**
Havfruen has a reputation as one of the finest restaurants in the city, and its menu offers an excellent range of fish and seafood dishes, (minimum of food miles guaranteed!), prepared in a variety of ways. Any diner finding the prospect of an eight-course meal prepared with the freshest ingredients a little too overwhelming can simply choose to miss out a few courses.

Kjøpmannsgata 7;
Tel 73 87 40 70;
Mon–Sat 18.00–24.00.
www.havfruen.no

❹ Primo
A taste of the Mediterranean in Scandinavia: this restaurant serves a remarkable selection of Italian dishes in an elegant atmosphere – naturally, accompanied by a carefully chosen range of fine wines. If in a hurry, you can order dishes to take away.

TMV-kaia 21; Tel 73 60 06 06;
Mon–Sat 11.00–23.00, Sun
12.00–22.00.
www.primorestaurant.no

Accommodation

❺ Britannia
This luxury hotel, opened in 1897, offers every comfort for a relaxing stay. All of its 247 rooms (including 11 suites) are equipped with an internet connection and cable TV. Palm trees and small fountains add to the stylish atmosphere of the Palmehaven restaurant, and the piano bar offers cocktails of every shape and size. The hotel also has an extensive spa area, containing a pool, a sauna, relaxation rooms, and a herbal bath.
Dronningensgate 5;
Tel. 73 80 08 00.
www.britannia.no

**❻ City Living
Schøller Hotel**
This hotel offers outstanding value for money. Its 50 rooms are attractively furnished, with bath, and vary in size. The friendly staff ensure that guests have a pleasant stay.
Dronningensgate 26;
Tel 73 87 08 00.
www.cityliving.no

Shopping

❼ Husfliden
Visitors on the hunt for souvenirs or Norwegian crafts will find plenty here, from traditional costumes to woodwork and glassware.
Olav Tryggvasonsgate 18;
Tel 73 83 32 30;
Mon–Fri 9.00–18.00, Sun
9.00–16.00.
www.norskflid.no/
trondheim

NORWAY EXPLORER

In Norway, the sea is never far away – the largest cities (such as Oslo and Bergen) are all situated along the coast and boast modern, well-equipped ports. Driving through Norway offers ample opportunity to see its beautiful countryside. Norway's roads take you through stunning fjord landscapes, past lakes nestling in the shadow of formidable mountain peaks, across plateaus with enormous glaciers, and through national parks boasting a rich variety of flora and fauna. Southern Norway is known for its charming small villages with white wooden houses and beautiful stave churches. A stopover at the North Cape is the high (and most distant) point of any visit.

Eating and drinking

1 **Solsiden**
This fish restaurant, lying below the fortress, is perhaps the best in Oslo – its seafood platter is positively legendary. The restaurant also offers a fairytale view of the port while the sun is setting.
Søndre Akershus Kai 34, Oslo; Tel 22 33 36 30; May–Aug 17.00–23.00 daily. www.solsiden.no

2 **N.B. Sørensens Dampskibsexpedition**
Located on the Stavanger waterfront, this is a great place to in which to enjoy a selection of tasty Scandinavian fare.
Skagen 26, 4006 Stavanger; Tel 51 84 38 20; Mon–Wed 11.00–24.00, Thurs–Sat 11.00–2.00, Sun 13.00–24.00. www.herlige-restauranter.no

Accommodation

3 **Mølla Hotell**
Lillehammer
A converted grain mill, the atmospere at the Mølla Hotell successfully combines modern with rustic. The view of Lillehammer from the top floor bar is probably the most spectacular to be found anywhere in the town.
Elvegaten 12, Lillehammer; Tel 61 05 70 80. www.mollahotell.no

4 **Kongsberg Vandrerhjem**
These comfortable lodgings, set in a beautiful location and open all year round, are well equipped and offer packages tailored to families and skiers.
Vinjesgate 1, Kongsberg; Tel 23 12 45 10. www. kongsberg-vandrerhjem.no

Sights

1 **Lillehammer**
Memorably the venue for the 1994 Winter Olympics, Lillehammer is more than just a Mecca for winter sports enthusiasts – it is a cultural stronghold. The Kunstmuseum exhibits famous works by Norwegian painters such as Edvard Munch, and the Maihaugen open-air museum is the largest in the country, consisting of around 180 separate buildings, including the Garmo stave church, built around 1150. (See also p. 68.)

2 **Hamar**
The Olympia Hall, better known as the Vikingskipet (the Viking Ship) thanks to its distinctive roof, is without a doubt the most famous landmark in this modern industrial town, situated on the eastern bank of Lake Mjøsa. The nearby Norsk Jerbanemuseum (the largest railway museum in Norway) exhibits a variety of historic locomotives, including magnificent saloon carriages.

3 **Oslo**
Norway's capital city is situated at the end of a fjord around 100 km (60 miles) inland. Between 1624 and 1924 Oslo was known as Kristiania. Although its inhabitants number barely half a million, Oslo is one of Europe's largest cities in terms of surface area and a hub for Norwegian trade and industry. Places of interest include the new City Hall with a richly decorated interior and fine church clock. Other sights include the fortress Akershus Festning, one of the country's most important medieval

buildings, the Nasjonalgalleriet containing a large collection of paintings and sculptures, and the Royal Palace. On the outskirts of the city is Holmenkollen, a winter sports location with a championship ski jump and a ski museum, and the Bygdøy museum peninsula, where you will find five museums: the Vikingskipshuset (Viking Ship Museum), the Fram Museum (polar exploration), the Norwegian Maritime Museum, the Norwegian Folk Museum, and finally the Kon-Tiki Museum. (See also p. 60.)

4 **Larvik**
The port of Larvik is known for its abundant natural springs, as well for giving its name to the mineral Larvikite, which is mined in various quarries around the town. Larvik's church contains a portrait of Martin Luther, painted by Lucas Cranach the Elder.

5 **Kristiansand**
This university city is a popular summer tourist destination. In the Kvadraturen (inner city), so-called because of its grid-like layout, a number of quaint old houses have been carefully restored. Kristiansand was founded during the 17th century by King Christian IV, and subsequently named after him. The city holds a number of festivals throughout the year, including the Bragdøya Blues Festival in June, and the Quart Festival, the largest music festival in Norway.

6 **Stavanger**
Situated on the Boknafjord, and almost 900 years old, Stavanger's economy was based on the fish processing industry until World War II,

when increased competition from abroad led to a decline. In 1970, the discovery of significant oil reserves in the Ekofisk oil field transformed Stavanger, the third largest city in Norway, into its oil-producing capital. Attractions include the Norsk Hermetikk Museum (Canning Museum), the old district of Gamle Stavanger with numerous tiny wooden houses lining cobbled alleyways and Stavanger's stone cathedral, the oldest in Norway. The Kongsgaard was the King of Denmark's Norwegian residence from the 14th to the 19th century. The

Valbergtårnet was built as a fire watchtower and is now one of Stavanger's principal landmarks. The eight-sided tower is visible from some distance and offers fine views over the city. (See also p. 20.)

From left: Hardangervidda National Park; 18th-century wooden houses line the streets in Gamle Stavanger; Lillehammer's ski pistes, used for the 1994 Winter Olympic Games.

LILLEHAMMER TO KONGSBERG

This touring route heads south from Lillehammer and runs through southern Norway. After leaving Oslo, it continues alongside the Oslofjord and Skagerrak, past Stavanger, and across Europe's largest plateau, heading east and north-east as far as Kongsberg, the final destination. Allow about a week.

7 Hardangervidda National Park
Europe's largest plateau provides fantastic scenery for hikers and a home for a great variety of animals, including some rare species. The protected national park area makes up around a third of the Hardangervidda, which is dotted with abundant lakes. (See also p. 30.)

8 Eidsborg
This region's most important attraction is its 13th-century stave church, one of the best preserved examples in the country. Unusually, the roof is entirely covered with wooden shingles, which is not typical for the area.

9 Heddal
The province of Telemark is home to Norway's largest stave church. Completed in 1242, it has a triple nave and features a svalgang (a kind of verandah-style shelter), which served both as protection from the

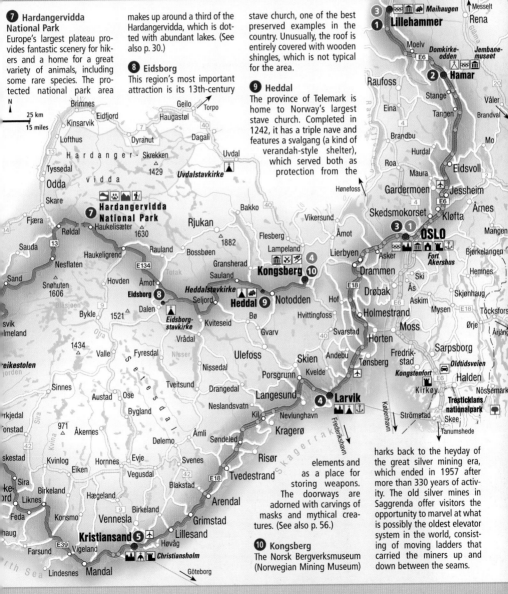

10 Kongsberg
The Norsk Bergverksmuseum (Norwegian Mining Museum)

harks back to the heyday of the great silver mining era, which ended in 1957 after more than 330 years of activity. The old silver mines in Saggrenda offer visitors the opportunity to marvel at what is possibly the oldest elevator system in the world, consisting of moving ladders that carried the miners up and down between the seams.

elements and as a place for storing weapons. The doorways are adorned with carvings of masks and mythical creatures. (See also p. 56.)

Sights

❶ Bergen

Bergen is Norway's second largest city after Oslo. It was founded in 1070 and served as the king's primary residence. Bergen experienced remarkable growth from the middle of the 14th century onward, after the Hanseatic League arrived – it was the most important port on the North Sea coast for centuries. The district of Bryggen (Norwegian for wharf) is a UNESCO World Heritage Site noted for its old Hanseatic warehouses, often brightly painted – one of them houses the Hanseatic Museum. Other attractions include Bergen's fishing port, the cathedral dating from the 13th century, the 12th-century Mariakirken (St Mary's Church, the oldest building in the city), the Bergenhus Festning (fortress), and the open-air Gamle Bergen Museum. The bustling Bergen fish market draws both locals and tourists in droves to see the wide range of fresh fish on offer. (See also pp. 32, 34.)

❷ Viksøyri and Sognefjord

Viksøyri is a tiny village on the Sognefjord, famous for its well-preserved stave church. The fjord is 204 km (127 miles) long and reaches depths of over 1,300 m (4,250 feet). (See also p. 38.)

❸ Stalheimskleiva and Nærøyfjord

The Stalheimskleiva mountain road winds its way through the landscape in a series of curves, reaching gradients of up to 18 percent. The Nærøyfjord, a southern branch of the Sognefjord, is the narrowest in the country – it measures just 250 m (820 feet) across at its widest point, and during the winter, the sun remains hidden behind its almost vertical rock walls. Beside the road, two impressive waterfalls plunge down the mountain into the fjord – the Stalheimfoss (126 m or 413 feet) and the Sivlefoss (240 m or 787 feet).

❹ Borgund

Norway's best preserved stave church was constructed around 1180, and is famous for its wealth of decorative carvings. Inside its walls are covered with elaborate mythical creatures and human heads. The ancient runic inscriptions, now protected behind special covers, are particularly interesting. A pagoda-like bell tower is next to the church. Like the majority of stave churches, the beautiful

BERGEN TO OPPDAL

This tour starts at the historic city of Bergen, and continues around stunning fjords and between spectacular mountain ranges. The landscape is characterized by mighty glaciers and waterfalls, which cascade down the mountainside. The route also takes in towns and cities and beautiful stave churches. Allow eight to ten days.

Borgund church was built some distance from the nearest settlement. The tourist office provides information on the architecture and history of stave churches.

5 Urnes
The eastern bank of the Lustrafjord is home to the 11th-century Urnes stave church, the oldest of Norway's 29 remaining stave churches (and a UNESCO World Heritage Site). The old portal in the northern wall is famous for its beautiful carved decoration, which includes mythical creatures intertwined – from dragons and lions to snakes. The church has given its name to this style of decoration, known as "Urnes-style", which was prevalent in the 11th and 12th centuries. Animals are portrayed in stylized form, with slender bodies and limbs and almond-shaped eyes. (See also p. 40.)

6 Jotunheimen National Park and Sognefjell National Route
Norway's highest and most spectacular mountain pass runs between the towns of Sogndal and Lom. It snakes up in a series of steep bends through the Jotunheimen mountain range, where 200 or more mountains are over 2,000 m (6,500 feet) high, the two highest being Galdhøppigen (2,469 m/8,100 feet) and Glittertind (2,452 m/8,045 feet). Numerous lakes are scattered about the Sognefjell plateau. Mainland Europe's largest glacier, the Jostedalsbreen, stretches into the distance to the west of the pass. Around 100 km (62 miles) in length, it covers approximately 500 sq. km (190 sq. miles), and

the ice is up to 500 m (1,640 feet) thick in places, with more than 20 glacier tongues flowing out into the surrounding tributary valleys. A number of hiking trails follow the perimeter of this immense body of ice. The National Park office in Jostedal provides information about the glacier and trails. (See also p. 72.)

7 Geirangerfjord
The Geirangerfjord, a branch of the Sunnylvsfjord is around 15 km (9 miles) long. Many waterfalls, including the Bridal Veil and the Suitor, cascade down its sides (up to 800 m/2,600 feet high) into the fjord. The view from the Dalsnibba observation point overlooking the Geirangerfjord is also spectacular. The Ørneveien (Eagle Way) winds its way up into the mountains and offers even more wonderful views over the fjord. As the road climbs, abandoned farm buildings come into view, some perched breathtakingly close to the steep rocky cliffs and now virtually inaccessible. The strong sunlight here meant that the cultivation of crops was fairly lucrative, despite the difficulties of the terrain. The Geirangerfjord was declared a UNESCO World Heritage Site in 2005. (See also p. 44.)

8 Ålesund
The city covers several islands, with its center located on Aspøy and Nørvøy. Ålesund is a seaport and one of the most important fishing ports in Norway. Atlanterhavsparken aquarium contains a variety of the marine flora and fauna found along the Norwegian coast. Ålesund is characterized by its stone houses (not typical of Nor-

way), built in the art nouveau style by architects brought in from Europe following a devastating fire that ravaged the city in 1904. The city's many attractions include Aksla (189 m/620 feet), a small mountain accessible from the city's park, from where there is a great view of the city, the skerry island fringe, and also the Sunnmøre Mountains to the west. To the east of the city, the open-air Sunnmøre Museum consists of more than 40 residential and farm buildings. (See also p. 46.)

9 Dovrefjell
This mountain region is one of Norway's most striking landscapes. The plateau is the highest point on the tour, crowned by the 2,286-m (7,500-foot) high Snøhetta, from where there are some fantastic views. Most of the Dovrefjell area is now protected as two national parks. They include the only intact high mountain ecosystem remaining in Europe. It provides a natural habitat for rare plants and animals – musk oxen have even been successfully introduced here from Greenland and guided hikes allow visitors to get close to the animals. The Kongsvold Fjellstue botanical garden contains alpine plants from other regions. (See also p. 102.)

10 Oppdal
In the foothills of the Dovrefjell, Oppdal is the starting point for tours to one of Norway's largest continuous skiing regions. The Oppdal open-air museum contains numerous buildings (including houses, sheds, stables, and mills) and a collection of around 2,000 objects. There is also an exhibition of local textiles.

Eating and drinking

1 Hotelrestaurant Stalheim
This restaurant, also containing a bar and a coffee lounge, is situated right next to the magical Nærøyfjord with picture postcard views. Inside, the rooms are decorated with antiques.
Stalheim Hotel, Stalheim;
Tel 56 52 01 22;
May until early Oct
Mon–Sun.
www.stalheim.com

2 Sjøbua
A fish restaurant situated on Ålesund's waterfront. Its ingredients are sourced directly from the catch of the day.
Brunholmgata 1A, Ålesund;
Tel 70 12 71 00;
Mon–Fri 16.00–1.00.
www.sjoebua.no

Accommodation

3 Thon Hotel Sandviken Brygge
In a perfect Bergen location, this modern hotel is one of a chain and has a well-equipped spa area offering a variety of treatments. The rooms are decorated with artworks.
Sandviksveien 94, Bergen;
Tel 55 39 61 00.
www.thonhotels.com/
sandvikenbrygge

4 Hotel Nor
Convenient for the nearby ski slopes, as well as for exploring Oppdal, this hotel has a restaurant, salon, and bar, and well-furnished rooms, 15 of which have a balcony. There is a steam room to ease aching limbs after a day on the pistes.
Aunevegen 6, Oppdal;
Tel 72 40 47 00.
www.oppdalbooking.no

Sights

❶ Trondheim

Over 1,000 years old, Trondheim was the capital of Norway in the Middle Ages – the Norwegian monarchy are still crowned here in Nidaros Cathedral. This magnificent building was erected over the grave of Olav the Holy in 1070. Richly decorated with sculptures, its west front is particularly spectacular. The Tyholt telecommunications tower, the Kristiansten fortress, and the tower belonging to the cathedral all provide great views over the rooftops of the city. (See pp. 96, 182.)

❷ Mosjøen

Picturesque Sjøgata Street, lined with brightly painted, 19th-century wooden houses, is this town's main attraction. The Vefsn Museum displays works by contemporary artists.

❸ Mo i Rana and Grønligrotta

The town museum offers an excellent insight into Sami life and culture. To the north of Mo i Rana, the Gronligrotta cave system, with an impressive display of stalactites, can be visited on guided tours.

❹ Svartisen

Svartisen ("black ice"), the second largest glacier in Norway after Jostedalsbreen, is one of the area's biggest attractions. Part of the Saltfjellet-Svartisen National Park, in some places the glacier stretches as far as the coast. (See also p. 120.)

Eating and drinking

❶ Søilen

This restaurant is part of the Meyergården Hotel in Mo i Rana, and focuses particularly on traditional local cuisine featuring seasonal produce. Their special dish is reindeer, prepared in every way that you could imagine.
Fridtjof Nansens gate 28, Mo i Rana; Tel 75 13 40 00; 7.00–24.00 daily. www.meyergarden.no

❷ Steakers

As the name would suggest, a steakhouse offering a great alternative to Tromsø's many fish restaurants. Diners can enjoy a fine view of the port while enjoying their meal.
Frederik Langes gate 13, Tromsø; Tel 77 61 33 30; Mon–Sat 15.00–23.00, Sun 14.00–22.00. www.steakers.no

Accommodation

❸ Sommerhotell Singsaker

The cozy atmosphere and peaceful surroundings of the large wooden building that houses this Trondheim hotel make it particularly special. It is excellent value for money, and boasts a large garden.
Rogertsgate 1, Trondheim; Tel 73 89 31 00. www.sommerhotell.singsaker.no

❹ Arran Nordkapp

This has to be one of the most northerly hotels in Europe. The Hotel Arran Nordkapp is really part of Kamøyvær, but lies outside the village. The majority of its comfortable rooms offer a sea view.
Tel 78 47 51 29. www.arran.as

TRONDHEIM TO THE NORTH CAPE

This tour showcases the delightful coastal scenery of the north of the country, with possible detours including a visit to the Lofoten Islands. The tour finishes at (almost) the most northerly point in Europe. To ensure you don't miss out on any of the sights on offer, allow at least ten days for this trip.

⑤ Arctic Circle
The Polarsirkelsenteret (Arctic Circle Center), where "Arctic Circle Certificates" are available, is open from May until mid-September, and is located directly on the Arctic Circle. The Center includes an information bureau, a restaurant, and a souvenir shop. (See also p. 122.)

⑥ Narvik
An ice-free port on the Ofotfjord, Swedish iron ore from Kiruna is exported to the rest of the world from Narvik. To the east, toward the border with Sweden, mountains dominate the landscape, including Fagernessfjell (656 m/2,152 feet high). Trips to the Lofoten Islands run from Narvik. (See also p. 118.)

⑦ Lofoten
This archipelago, situated just off the coast of the Norwegian mainland, is made up of around 80 islands, connected by a series of bridges and tunnels. The Lofoten Islands are set apart by their craggy mountain peaks with steep rocky faces, lush green meadows, and brightly painted wooden houses mounted on stilts. Thanks to the warm-

ing warming waters of the Gulf Stream, the climate in this remote area of Europe is unusually mild. (See also p. 8.)

⑧ Tromsø
The largest city in northern Norway boasts a mild climate – the Tromsø palm, which loves the warmth, flourishes here. The Tromsøbrua (Tromsø Bridge) has a span of 1,036 m (3,399 feet) and links the city with the mainland. Tromsø's main landmark is its distinctive Arctic Cathedral, which was completed in 1965. It has a large stained glass window, 23 m (75 feet) high and occupying the entire eastern wall. The Polar Museum explains all there is to know about international polar expeditions. (See also p. 140.)

⑨ Alta
Situated on the fjord of the same name, Alta is a stronghold of Sami culture, and the Hjemmeluft rock carvings which are between 2,000

and 6,000 years old are particularly worth seeing. They depict animals, as well as scenes of hunting and daily life, and have been designated a World Heritage Site. The Alta Canyon also attracts many visitors. It is over 15 km (9 miles) long and up to 500 m (1640 feet) deep. (See also p. 138.)

⑩ Hammerfest
Hammerfest is one of the most northerly settlements in the world, and the starting point for fishing trips (both commercial and sport) on the Norwegian Sea. The Meridian Monument, erected in 1854, commemorates the first

successful attempt to measure the Earth's radius.

⑪ North Cape
Tours run from the mainland to Honningsvåg on the North Cape island of Magerøya. The two are also connected by a road tunnel beneath the sea. Although generally overcast, the North Cape is heavily marketed to tourists. Despite not actually being the most northerly point in Europe, the North Cape is well worth a visit. (See also p. 130.)

January

Northern Lights Festival

Tromsø. Mid-winter is the best time to see the phenomenon of the Northern Lights in all their magnificent glory – as you travel further north, the bright haze that lights up the night hours dances increasingly spectacularly across the sky. In Tromsø, to the north of the Arctic Circle, the spectacular light effects have inspired a major film festival. It is the most northerly (and indeed probably the coldest) in the world and features productions from regions near the Arctic, including Canada, Russia, and the Scandinavian countries. The events of the festival compensate for the extreme climatic conditions that emerge at this time of year, when Tromsø enjoys no more than a single hour of daylight. As well as numerous films, the Northern Lights Festival also offers a wonderful variety of musical performances, ranging from classical music to jazz.
Tel 77 61 00 00;
mid-Jan.
www.destinasjontromso.no

March

Holmenkollen ski festival

Oslo. This is an absolutely unmissable event for winter sports fans, as world records are regularly smashed here: the world elite of Nordic skiing all pass though the gates of the Norwegian capital to compete in the disciplines of ski-jumping, cross-country skiing, Nordic combined, and biathlon. These events have evolved over more than a century, as tournaments have been taking place here since 1892. The wide expanse of Holmenkollen mountain has already hosted several world championships, as well as the 1952 Winter Olympic Games. Tens of thousands of visitors transform this ski festival into an enthusiastic celebration of folk culture.
Tel 22 92 32 00;
early Mar.
www.holmenkollen-worldcup.no

March/April

Sami Easter celebrations

Kautokeino. Easter time heralds lively festivities for the Sami people (also known as Lapps) every year, when they celebrate the end of the long, cold winter and the arrival of the reindeer-grazing season. This time of year is particularly spectacular in the "reindeer capital" of Kautokeino, home to around 3,000 people and 100,000 reindeer, where everyone is decked out in the brightest costumes imaginable during what are very energetic celebrations. Easter is also often a time for traditional weddings and baptisms, and tourists are warmly invited to join in. Reindeer sled racing is also extremely popular. The Sami Grand Prix awards prizes to the best performances of Joik (folksong), which never fail to captivate each and every visitor that hears them. The songs can sound sorrowful, angry, sad, melancholic or joyous. Songs usually have short lyrics or no lyrics at all and can be deeply personal or spiritual in nature. Improvisation is not unusual.
Tel 78 48 65 00;
Easter.
www.kautokeino.no

May

Bergen International Festival

Bergen. For two weeks every year, the country's second largest city is turned upside down by one of the most famous performing arts festivals in the whole of Scandinavia. There are concerts featuring classical and modern artists, traditional and experimental music, as well as drama performances and dance displays, which are staged in a variety of locations. The major venues include such prestigious cultural hotspots as the Haakonshallen, the Grieghallen, and Den National Scene (the National Venue of Theater) – all must-sees for any visitor. However, the events of the festival take place all over Bergen, and include street musicians along with other spontaneous cabaret performances. "Night Jazz Bergen" runs alongside the festival, with performances on many of the city's stages featuring the local and international greats of the jazz world. These two festivals combine to create a spectacular two weeks in the extreme north that would be hard to beat.
Tel 55 55 20 00;
late May/early Jun.
www.visitbergen.com

June

North Cape Festival

Honningsvåg. The extreme north has its very own special atmosphere, the result of a unique combination of peacefulness and a wide expanse of landscape. But even here, there are celebrations! A few days before the summer solstice every year, the south coast of Magerøya island (containing the North Cape itself) plays host to the Nordkappfestivalen, which attracts visitors in droves. Plays, concerts, exhibitions, a wide range of folk performances, and much more continue to delight and entertain audiences throughout the night, imperceptible though it is. Highlights of the festival include a huge ship parade.
Tel 78 47 70 30;
mid Jun.
www.nordkapp.no

Festival of North Norway

Harstad. Every year in the middle of summer, this small north Norwegian city invites visitors to enjoy its huge variety of cultural events – from music, drama, and dance to exhibitions and films, as well as readings and workshops. Well-known actors perform alongside lesser known talents and up-and-coming newcomers. The festival allows this otherwise rather introspective city to display its hugely lively side.
Tel 90 66 08 55;
late Jun.
www.festivalharstad.no
and www.festspillnn.no

Chamber Music Festival

Risør. This festival celebrating chamber music, established in 1991, boasts a wide repertoire that includes the classics and contemporary pieces, with other genres in between. Unlike many other events of this nature, the festival is not primarily a commercial exercise. Instead, the assembled musicians, including many new talented performers, spend the entire festival week in Risør and perform several times in various different line-ups, an

FESTIVAL CALENDAR

From the North Cape to Kristiansand on the south coast, Norway loves to celebrate. Cities such as Oslo and Bergen organize world-class music and drama festivals featuring ambitious performances, ranging from the classical to the modern, and the Midsummer Night festivities include a range of enjoyable and entertaining open-air events.

arrangement that gives the festival its own particular character. Every year, musicians from different ensembles and orchestras come together to form the Risør Festival Strings: this ensemble is only brought together for the duration of the festival, yet the muscians play together in perfect harmony.
Tel 37 15 32 50;
late Jun.
www.kammermusikkfest.no

July

Quart Festival
Kristiansand. Every July, this small city in northern Norway attracts a crowd of predominantly young people to an event lasting several days and featuring a variety of rock and pop stars. The festival's unique selling point is its diversity: performers include bands recognized as outstanding live performers, as well as a number of popular radio DJs – where else could you experience major rock icons such as The Who and polar opposite newcomers like Scissor Sisters performing in succession on the same stage? Many visitors stay at the campsite, located around 2 km (1.2 miles) away from the main festival area. As well as the concerts taking place on the outdoor stage, the Quart Festival hosts live music in various small clubs.
Tel 38 07 50 00;
early Jul.
www.quart.no

Moldejazz
Molde. Every July, Molde is transformed into a paradise for jazz enthusiasts. Norway's largest jazz festival, generally considered by many insiders to be the country's finest,

attracts hundreds of artists (both bands and soloists) to come and perform – whether in the concert hall, in a club, in a tent, in the church, or on the street. This festival (established in 1961) is proud to have welcomed such worldwide superstars as Miles Davis, Oscar Peterson, Herbie Hancock, Dizzy Gillespie, Chick Corea, and Pat Metheny. Various performances from the greats of blues, rock, and pop take place alongside the jazz festival, allowing visitors to Molde to experience live music from such blues and rock legends as B.B. King, Muddy Waters, Joe Cocker, and Carlos Santana between jazz concerts.
Tel 71 20 31 50;
mid-Jul.
www.moldejazz.no

The Battle of Stiklestad
Stiklestad. Here, history is brought to life to illustrate the events of this epic Norwegian struggle: the historically important battle of 1030, which sealed the Christianization of Norway, is re-enacted every July. Christian troops with King Olav Haraldsson at their head fought against an army led by heathen chieftains, and although King Olav (who was later canonized) was killed in the battle, the Christian forces still managed to triumph. On the anniversary of the battle, hundreds of actors and extras – naturally all with authentic clothing and weapons – re-enact this important event with much gusto (and even more noise).
Tel 74 04 42 00;
29 July.
www.stiklestad.no

August

Peer Gynt Festival
Vinstra. This ten-day festival focuses on Norwegian culture and poetry. There is no more authentic performance of the play Peer Gynt than the one that takes place here in the open air, as its creator Henrik Ibsen was inspired by the landscape of Vinstra when writing the Norwegian national epic. It was on a journey along the extensive valley of Gudbrandsdal in Oppland that Ibsen first heard the stories that gave him the inspiration for his most famous play, describing a young man's wild adventures, earning Ibsen a permanent place in the canon of world literature. The music of Edvard Grieg, the spectacular natural backdrop, and the melancholy of Norway's Midsummer Night all combine to make the performance a remarkable and truly unforgettable experience. The play is staged on every day of the festival, which also offers an ambitious series of concerts and literary seminars.
Tel 61 29 47 70;
early Aug.
www.peergynt.no

Øya Festival
Oslo. Both Norwegian bands and international acts add spice to this four-day celebration of indie, pop, and rock music. On every day of the festival, thousands of spectators stream into the Middelalderparken (Medieval Park) to watch performances on the festival's three outdoor stages. The park may be situated in the middle of Oslo but it feels more like a small, calm island (øya is Norwegian for island)

amid the bustle of the city, with medieval ruins that give a very special ambience. Although there is plenty going on and some bands can be heard from nearby parts of the city, the atmosphere is extremely relaxed. The already legendary Club Night takes place the evening before the festival starts, when around 30 of Oslo's clubs each host performances by between three to five bands, and the spectators get themselves loudly in the mood for the coming days.
Tel 48 09 19 48;
mid-Aug.
www.oyafestivalen.com

September

ULTIMA – Contemporary Music Festival
Oslo. This annual festival (founded in 1991) celebrates modern music and other related art forms, and is undoubtedly one of the most firmly established of its kind in Europe. Numbering between 80 and 100 in total, the concert venues are dotted all over the city, and range from venerable concert halls to casual clubs. The open-air stage area is scattered with installations and sculptures by contemporary artists. However, what makes ULTIMA such a special event is the huge number of world premieres it attracts and hosts, as well as the festival's innovative, and unique, character, reflecting the newest ideas and inspirations of the modern art scene. Composers whose works have been performed here in recent years include Luca Francesconi and Georg Friedrich Haas.
Tel 22 40 18 90;
mid-Sept.
www.ultima.no

The Helleren rock face on the Jøss-ingfjord, situated in the west coast community of Sokndal in Rogaland: people have been living in abris (rock shelters), situated 30 m (100 feet) high up the rock face and reaching 15 m (50 feet) into it in places, for thousands of years.

KEY

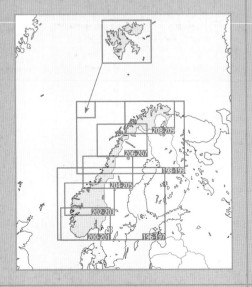

▬▬▬▬ ∷∷∷	Freeway (motorway) (under construction)
▬▬▬ ⁼⁼⁼⁼	Multi-lane expressway (under construction)
▬▬▬ ▪▪▪▪	Highway (trunk road)/National road (under construction)
▬▬▬	Arterial road (primary route)
▬▬▬	Major road/Local road
▪▪▪▪▪▪▪▪▪	National Tourist Route
╼╾╼╾╼	Tourist railroad (railway)
)▬▬▬(▬▬▬(	Road/Railroad tunnel
40 45 **23** E18	Arterial road (primary route) number/European road number
✈ ✈	International/Domestic airport
▬▬▬▬ ----	Ferry/Hurtigruten route
▬▪▬▪▬▪	International border
☐	National park boundary

ATLAS

The maps in the Atlas section give detailed practical information to help make your stay more enjoyable. Clear symbols indicate the position of buildings and monuments of note, facilities and services, public buildings, the transport network, and built-up areas and green spaces (see the key to the maps below).

🏛 Museum/Music/Theater	♣ Market/Shopping	🚶 Hiking area	🛶 Canoeing/Rafting
🎵 Festival	✗ Refreshments/Restaurant	⛺ Hiking accommodation	🏟 Stadium
🅿 Sports/Games/Leisure	🛏 Accommodation	🎿 Viewpoint	🅿 Leisure park
🏊 Health and fitness	ℹ Information	🚠 Cable car	🐎 Equestrian sport
		🎿 Ski area	
⬛ UNESCO Natural Heritage Site	🌲 Nature park		
🏔 Mountain landscape	🌳 National park (landscape)	🚗 Scenic car route	🚢 Shipping route
🏖 Coastal landscape	🌿 National park (plantlife)	🚂 Scenic railroad route	
🌊 Dunes	🏛 National park (cultural heritage)		
🏞 Lakeland	🐟 Aquarium	⬜ UNESCO World Heritage Site	⊕ World's fair (exhibition)
🏔 Glacier	🦅 Bird sanctuary	🚩 Viking culture	🏅 Olympic city
🕳 Cave	🦁 Game reserve	⛪ Christian culture site	🏛 Open-air museum
🏜 Canyon	🏖 Beach	⛪ Ruined church	🗼 Notable lighthouse
💦 Waterfall	🏝 Island	⛪ Gothic church	🗼 Notable tower
🦒 Zoo	🌊 Marine reserve	🎨 Cultivated landscape	🏭 Industrial monument
⚓ Port	🏖 Bathing resort	🗿 Prehistoric rock art	⛏ Mine (abandoned)
⛵ Sailing	♨ Spa/Hot springs	🏘 Historic town/city area	🏛 Monument/Tomb
🏄 Windsurfing	🤿 Diving (subaqua)	🏰 Castle/Fortress/Defenses	🗿 Memorial
		🏰 Palace/Castle	🎭 Theater

ARCTIC OCEAN

1248

Nordvest-
Spitsbergen
nasjonalpark

Sjuøyane

Snøtoppen
620 ▲

Gotha-
halvøya

Amsterdamøya

354 ▲

1130 ▲ Andrée-
1368 ▲ Land
Newtontoppen
1717

Kongsvegen
Kongbreen

Tre Kroner
1225

Ny Ålesund

1085 ▲

Prins Karls
Forland

997

Pyramiden

Hyperitt-
fossen

Longyearbyen
LYR

Isfjord
Radio

Barentsburg

Forlandet
nasjonalpark

Nordaust-Svalbard
naturreservat

Nordaustlandet

naturreservat

340 ▲

Wilhelmøya

Kvitøya ▲410

Storøya

Orvin Land

Nordaust-
Svalbard
naturreservat

Abeløya

Kongsøya
▲320

230 ▲
Svenskøya

665 ▲
Barentsøya
Søraust-

Kong Karls Land

Nordaust-
Svalbard
naturreservat

Svalbard

590 Edgeøya
naturreservat

67

SVALBARD

1205 ▲

Sør-Spitsbergen
nasjonalpark

Hornsundtind
1430

Øyrlandsodden

Sørkappøya

Kvalpynten ▲395

155

Hopen

Hopen Radio Kapp Thor
370

103

Barents Sea

N

0 ___ 80 km
40 miles

Lofoten Basin

3378

3070

Norwegian

Sea

3274

Vesterålen

Grylefjord
Andenes
ANX Senja

Andøya

Stonglandet Sjø
And-
fjorden

Myre

Harstad Hamnvik

Langøya

Sørtland

Steine

Hadseløya

Austvågøya

Vestvågøy

Leknes

Bøstad

Moskenesøya

Sørvågen

Værøy

Røst

Hinnøya

74 Grov

Stokmarknes

Bogen
EVE NVK
Ballangen

Lødingen

Svolvær
210

SVJ

Kabelvåg
Henningsvær
Stamsund

Ulvsvåg

Skarberget

Åstad 263

Steigen

Nordfold

Mørsvikfjorden
Mørsvik

Ritse

Mørsvik

Rago n.p.
Padjelanta
nasjonalpark

Røsvik

BOO
Løding

Bodø
Saltstraumen

Fauske

Stalo-
luokta
fjällstation

Stalo-
luokta

Suitjelma

Sulitjelma 1914

Kvikk
fjällsta

Kvikk

Vöring Plateau

NORWAY

125

Vesterli

Inndyr

Ørnes

Storjorda

Vågaholmen

Melfjorden

Stokkvågen

Tomma

Donna

Sandnessjøen

Vegaøyan

Vega
Gladstad

Tjøtta

Brønnøysund
BNN

Leka
Sør-Gutvika

Vikna
Valøy

Rørvik

RVK

Salsbruket

Høylandet

96
Halten Bank

Saltfjellet-
Svartisen
nasjonalpark

1594 ▲

Grønligrotta

MQN

Mo i Rana

Nesna

Hemnesberget
Korgen

1915

Bleikvasli

Forvika Vevelstad

Trofors

Tosbotn

Holm

Terråk

Namsskogan

Skorovatn

178
Storjord

77 Stødi

93

E06

Pieljekaise
nationalpark

Jä

Silverm

Ammarnäs

Hemavan

Västansjø

Hattfjelldal

1703 ▲
Ivarrud

241

Tärnaby

Sor

Slussfors

Kittelfjäll

Långsjöby

Saxnäs

Risbäck

Börgefjell
nasjonalpark

448

Trappstegsforsarna

92

N

0 ___ 40 km
20 miles

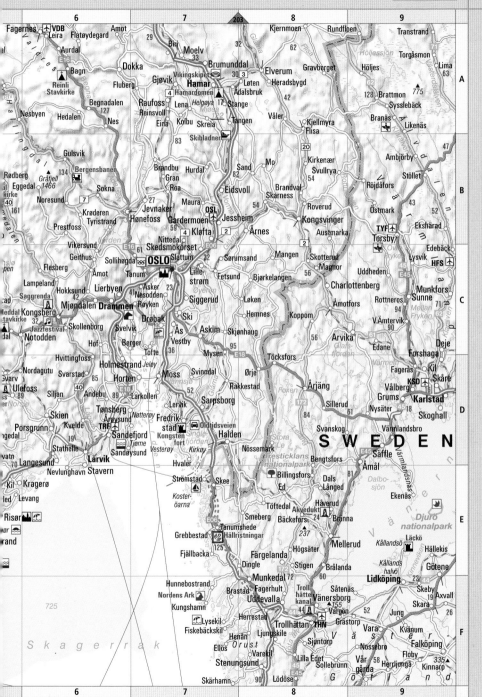

N

0   20 km
10 miles

N o r w e g i a n

S e a

GI
Ve
Vegaøy

Ven

Leka   Skei
Sør-Gutvik

Valøy
Vikna   **RVK**   Rørvik   Kolve
Salsbruke
96   Abelvær   Lund
Halten Bank   *Joa*
Utvorda   *Otterøya*
   Hamnes
Sør-Flatanger   Ranem
   Namsos   17
   OSY

Osen   Sjøasen   Bangsund

N O R W A Y

Hofstad
   Finnvollheia   Tørring   68
Harsvika   675   Malm
    Follafors   Bølareinen   Skj
Lysøysundet   Å   Steinkjer
   516   28
   Straumen   Sparbu
Hellesvikan   Verdalsøra
Frøya   Rødsjøen
Titran   Hammarvika   Brekstad   Botngård   *Ytterøy*   Skogn   Vuku
    Leksvik   Levanger
Fillan   Valset   Rissa   53
Frøyfjorden
Hitra   Sandstad   Vanvikan   Frosta   Markabygd
Dyrnes   Hopen   Krå
   Forsnes   Selbekken   Rørvika   Skatval   Okkelberg   9C
Smøla   Stjørdal   71
   Snillfjord   Vikhammer   **TRB**   Merå
Kørsvoll   **Trondheim**   Hommelvik   Ko
Vinsternes   Heimdal   15
Tustna   Leira   Aure   Kyrksæterøra   29   Orkanger   Klæbu   Storli
  Ertvågøy   Vinje   **E39**   49   Fannrem   Melhus   Okstad

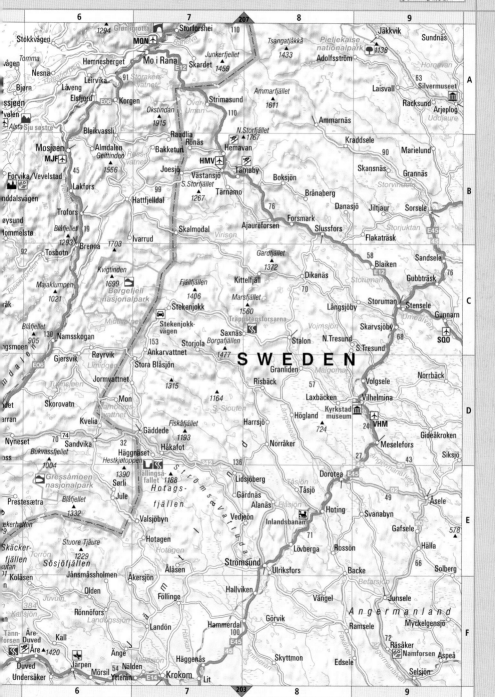

N

0   20 km
    10 miles

Norwegian

3070

Sea

Andene
Bleik
Andøya
Nordmela
My
90
Risøyhamn   Grø
Myre
Langøya   Myrland
Sortland   Flesnes   R
Straumsnes   32
Steine   74   *Hin*
Stokmarknes   Møysalen   Gullesfjo
Hadseløya   SKN   ▲
Melbu   1262   E10
Hanøy 50 Lødingen
Fiskebøl   ▲1146
Rindbø
Vestvågøy   Austvågøya   Digermulen
135   Svolvær   Ska
LKN   ↑SVJ   Bogne
↑Leknes   Kabelvåg   Tranøya
Flakstad   Stamsund — Henningsvær   Hamarøya   Ul
Ballstad   Skutvika   Presteid
Moskenesøya   Flakstadøya   Engeløya   Sk
Reine   Steigen   Åstad   Finnøya
Sørvågen   Tømn

Nordfold   Mørsvik
Helnessund   Mørsvik
Værøy   Sørland   Laukvika   Rein
Folda   1361   160
RET↑   Røst   Tårnvika   El
Misten   Røsvik
Helligvær   Landegode   Festvåg   asjon
63   E06
Straume
Bodø   80
BOO↑   Løding
Saltstraumen   Straumen   Fauske
Sandhornøy
Horsdal   Rognan   Su
Fugløya   Inndyr   Tverrvika   Vesterli   61   Nuc

NOR W ▲A Y
1405

123   Balvat
Ørnes
Meløya   Glomfjord   Ørfjellet Storjord 170
Åmnøya   Forøya   Leirmoen   1751   77
Vågaholmen   Storjorda   Saltfjellet-
Ågskardet   Svartisen   Saltfjellet   Guik
Snøtinden   nasjonalpark
Nesøya   1594 1572   1416   12
Jektvika   Stødi
Trænstaven   Melfjorden   Svar
Kilboghamn   Grønligrotta   Nasafjället
Lurøya   1294   Storforshei   110 1210
Stokkvågen   MON↑   Tsangatjåkk
Mo i Rana   1433▲

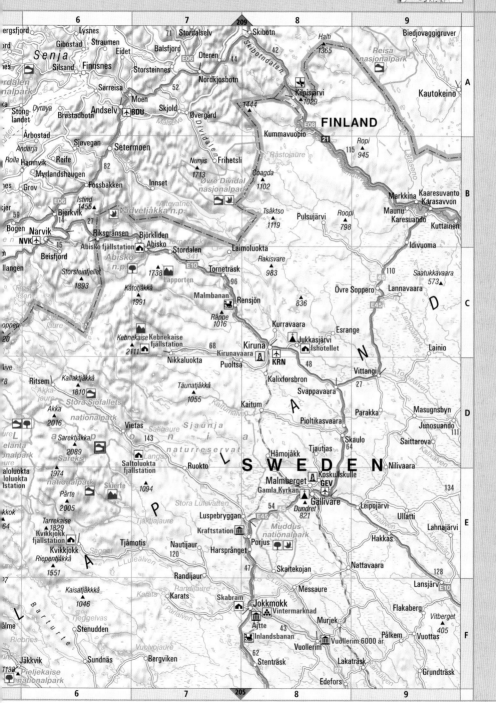

6 · **7** · **209** · **8** · **9**

ergsfjord · Lysnes · 71 Stordalselv · Skibotn · Halti · Biedjovaggigruver
rd · Gibostad · Straumen · Balsfjord · Oteren · 42 · 1365 · Reisa
Senja · Eidet · E06 · 44 · nasjonalpark
es · Silsand · Finnsnes · Storsteinnes · Nordkjosbotn · **A**
rdalen · Sørreisa · 52 · Kilpisjärvi · Kautokeino
nalpark · Moen · 1029
xa · Stong- Dyrøya · Andselv · BDU · Skjold · Øvergård · 1444
landet · Brøstadbotn · Målselv · E08 · **FINLAND**
Årbostad · Kummavuopio
Andørja · Sjøvegan · Setermoen · Råstojaure · 21 · Ropi
Rolla Hamnvik · Reife · 82 · Nunjis · Frihetsli · 115 · 945
Myrlandshaugen · 1713 · Coagda
es · Grov · Fossbakken · Innset · Øvre Dividal · 1102
nasjonalpark · Markkina · Kaaresuvanto · **B**
jer · E06 · Istind · Allevatnet · Tsåktso · Pulsujärvi · Roopi · Maunu · Karasavvon
59 · Bjerkvik · 1456 · Vadvetjåkka n.p. · 1119 · 798 · Karesuando
Bogen · Narvik · 14 · 27 · Riksgränsen · Björkliden · Kuttainen
NVK · 15 · Abisko fjällstation · Abisko · Stordalen · Laimoluokta · Idivuoma
n · Beisfjord · Abisko · 341 · Rakisvare
llangen · n.p. · 1738 · Torneträsk · 983 · 110 · Saatukkavaara
Storsteinfjellet · E10 · Lapporten · 96 · Övre Soppero · Lannavaara · 573
1893 · Kåtotjåkkå · Malmbanan · Rensjön · 836 · E45 · **C**
oppen · 1991 · Råppe · Kurravaara · Esrange
20 · Kebnekaise Kebnekaise · 1016 · Jukkasjärvi
2111 · fjällstation · 68 · **Kiruna** · Ishotellet · Lainio
åive · Nikkaluokta · Puoltsa · KRN · 48
8 · Ritsem · Kallaktjåkkå · Kirunavaara · Vittangi · 27
Akka- · 1810 · Täunatjåkkå · Kalixforsbron
jaure · Stora Sjöfallets · 1055 · Svappavaara · Masugnsbyn · **D**
Akka · nationalpark · Kaitum · Parakka
2016 · Vietas · Satihaure · **Sjaunja** · Pioltikasvaara · Junosuando
ureL · Sarektjåkkå · 143 · naturreservat · Skaulo · 111
elanta · 2089 · Saltoluokta · Håmojåkk · Tjautjas · 64 · Saittarova
nalpark · Sareks · fjällstation · Ruokto · **SWEDEN** · Nilivaara
aloluokta · 1974 · Langas · Koskullskulle
loluokta · nationalpark · Skierfe · 1094 · **Malmberget** · GEV
lstation · Pårte · Gamla Kyrkan · 134
kkok · 2005 · Stora Lulevatten · 54 · Dundret · Gällivare · Leipojärvi
64 · Tarrekaise · Tjaktjajaure · Luspebryggan · E45 · 821 · Ullatti · **E**
Kvikkjokk · 1829 · Kraftstation · Muddus · Lahnajärvi
fjällstation · Tjåmotis · Nautijaur · nationalpark · Hakkas
Kvikkjokk · 120 · Harsprånget · Porjus · Nattavaara · 128
Riepentjåkkå · Randijaur · 47 · Skaitekojan
1551 · Randijaure · Messaure · Lansjärv · E10
Kaisatjåkkå · Karats · Karats · Skabram · **Jokkmokk** · Flakaberg
1046 · Pärlälven · Vintermarknad · Murjek · Vitberget
älme · Tjeggelvas · Ajtte · 43 · Pålkem · 405 · Vuottas · **F**
Riebnes · Stenudden · Inlandsbanan · Vuollerim · Vuollerim 6000 år · Lakaträsk
Jäkkvik · Sundnäs · Bergviken · 62 · Stenträsk · Grundträsk
113 · Pieljekaise · Edefors
nationalpark

6 · **7** · **205** · **8** · **9**

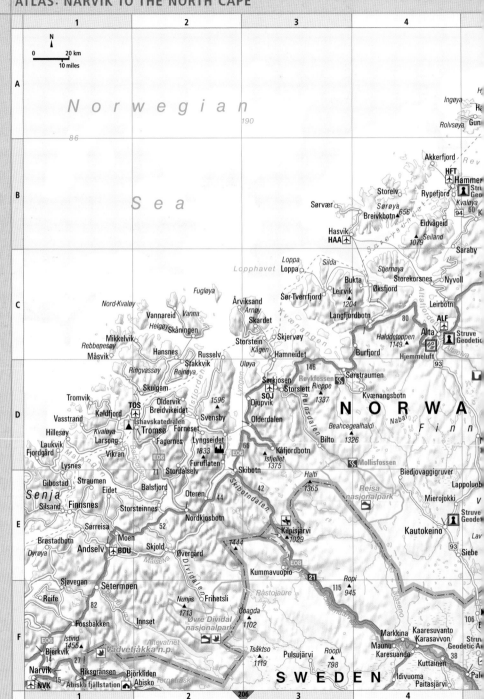

N

0   20 km
10 miles

1 | **2** | **3** | **4**

A

N o r w e g i a n

190

86

Ingøya

Ha

Rolvsøya   Gun

Akkerfjord   *Rev*

HFT
Hammer

B

S e a

Storelv
Sørvær   Rypefjord   Str
Geo

Sørøya   Kvaløya
Breivkbotn   656   94   60   K

Eidvågeid

Hasvik
HAA   Seiland
1079

Saraby

Loppa   *Silda*   Stjernøya   Nyvoll
Lopphavet Loppa   Storekorsnes
Bukta   Leirvik   Økstjord

C   Nord-Kvaløy   Fugløya   Årviksand   Sør-Tverrfjord   1204   Leirbotn
Arnøy   Langfjordbotn   80   ALF
Vannareid *Vanna*   Skardet
Helgøy Skåningen   Skjervøy   Halddetoppen   Alta   Struve
Storstein   1149   Geodetic
Mikkelvik   Kågen   Hamneidet   Burfjord
Rebbenesøy   Hansnes   Russelv   Hjemmeluft   93
Måsvik   Stakkvik   Uløya   146   Sørstraumen
Ringvassøy   Reinøya   Sørkjosen   Røykfossen   Sørstraumen
Skulgam   Storslett *Rieppe*
Tromvik   SOJ   1337   Kvænangsbotn
TOS   Oldervik   1596   Djupvik

D   Kåldfjord   Breidvikeidet   Svensby   Olderdalen   **N O R W A**
Vasstrand   Ishavskatedralen   Forneset   Beahcegealhaldi   *Naba*   *Finn*
Hillesøy   Kvaløya   Tromsø   Fagernes   Lyngseidet   66   Bilto   1326
Laukvik   Larseng   1833   E06   Isfjellet   Mollisfossen
Fjordgård   Vikran   Furuflaten   1375
Lysnes   71   Stordalselv   Skibotn   Halti   Biedjovaggigruver
Gibostad   Straumen   Balsfjord   Oteren   42   1365   Lappluob
Senja   Eidet   44   *Reisa*   Mierojokki   V
Silsand   Finnsnes   Storsteinnes   *nasjonalpark*   Struve
Nordkjosbotn   Geode

E   Sørreisa   52   Kilpisjärvi   Kautokeino   Lav
Brøstadbotn   Moen   1029   93
Dyrøya   Andselv   Skjold   T444   Siebe
BDU   Øvergård
Malselv   *Dividalen*   Kummavuopio   E08
21   Ropi
Sjøvegan   Setermoen   115   945
Reife   82   Nunjis   Frihetsli   *Råstojaure*
1713   Coagda
Fossbakken   Innset   *Øvre Divida*   1102   106
nasjonalpark
F   E06   Istind   Altevatnet   Markkina   Kaaresuvanto
1455   Maunu   Karasavvon   Stru
Bjerkvik   27   Vadvetjåkka n.p.   Tsåktso   Roopi   Karesuando   Geodetic
14   1119   Pulsujärvi   798   Kuttainen   38
Narvik   Idivuoma   Pal
NVK   Riksgränsen   Björkliden   **S W E D E N**   Paitasjärvi
Abisko fjällstation   Abisko   *Tornetråsk*

1 | **2** | 206 | **3** | **4**

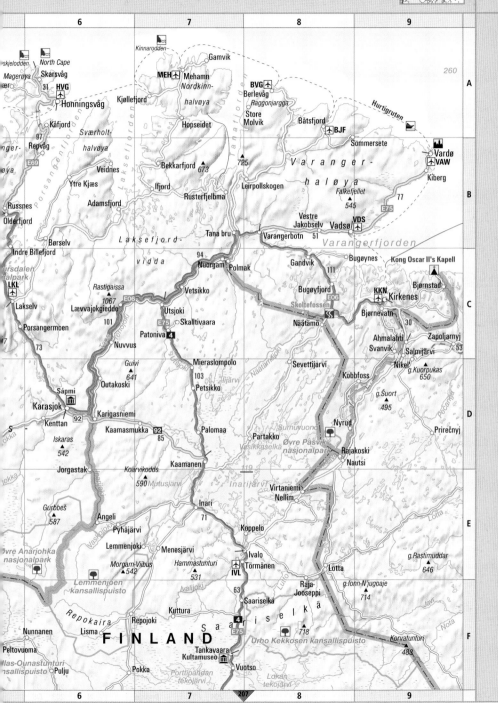

skjelodden North Cape
Magerøya Skarsvåg
ær 31 HVG⊞
Honningsvåg Kjøllefjord
Kåfjord Sværholt-
nger- Repvåg halvøya
øya E69
Veidnes
Ytre Kjæs
Russnes Adamsfjord
Olderfjord
Børselv
Indre Billefjord

Kinnarodden Gamvik
MEH⊞ Mehamn
Nordkinn-
halvøya
Hopseidet
Bekkarfjord▲ 673
Ifjord
Rusterfjelbma

Store
Molvik
725
Leirpollskogen

BVG⊞
Berlevåg
Raggonjargga
Båtsfjord
⊞BJF
Sommersete

Hurtigruten

260

Vardø
⊞VAW
Kiberg

V a r a n g e r -
h a l ø y a
Falkefjellet
▲
545
77
E75

A

Vestre
Jakobselv Vadsø VDS
⊞
Laksefjord- Tana bru Varangerbotn 51 Varangerfjorden

vidda 94
Nuorgam Polmak
LKL Rastigaissa Vetsikko
⊞ ▲
Lakselv 1067 E06 Utsjoki
Lævvajokgiedde E75 Skalltivaara
Porsangermoen 101
Patoniva 4
Nuvvus
Guivi Mieraslompolo
▲
641 103
Outakoski Petsikko
Sápmi
Karasjok 血
Kenttan 92
Karigasniemi
Iskaras Kaamasmukka 92
▲ 85 Palomaa
542
Jorgastak Koarvikodds
590 Mutusjärvi Kaamanen
Gurbbeš
▲ Inari
587 Angeli 71
Pyhäjärvi
Lemmenjoki Menesjärvi
Øvre Anárjohka Morgam-Viibus Hammastunturi
nasjonalpark ▲542 531
Lemmenjoen ⊞
kansallispuisto IVL
Ivalljoki
Repokaira Repojoki Kuttura
Nunnanen Lisma
Peltovuoma F I N L A N D
llas-Ounastunturi Tankavaara
nsallispuisto Pulju Pokka Kultamuseo 血
Porttipahdan
tekojärvi

Gandvik Bugøynes Kong Oscar II's Kapell
111
Bugøyfjord KKN Bjørnstad
E06 ⊞ Kirkenes
Skoltefossen
Näätämö Bjørnevatn
30
Ahmalahti Zapoljarnyj
Svanvik Salmijärvi 53
Sevettijärvi Nikel g.Kuorpukas
Kobbfoss 650
g.Suort
495
Surnuvuono Nyrud
Øvre Pasvik Prirečnyj
Vasikkaselkä nasjonalpark Rajakoski
Partakko Nautsi
119
Virtaniemi
Nellim
Koppelo
Ivalo g.Rastimuddar
Törmänen ▲
Lotta 646
63 Raja- g.fonn-N'jugoaje
Saariselkä Jooseppi 714
ä
Saariselkä
4 Urho Kekkosen kansallispuisto Korvatunturi
E75 718 488
Vuotso Lokan
tekojärvi

B

C

D

E

F

6 7 207 8 9

ATLAS: PLACES INDEX

Pages 198–209

Name				Name				Name			
Drøbak	N	201	C7	Farestad	N	200	F4	**G**äddede	S	205	D7
Duesund	N	202	E2	Farsund	N	200	F3	Gällivare	S	207	E8
Duved	S	205	F5	Fauske	N	206	E4	Gärdnäs	S	205	E7
Dyranut	N	200	B4	Fåvang	N	203	E6	Gafsele	S	205	E9
Dyrnes	N	204	F1	Feda	N	200	F3	Gamvik	N	209	A7
				Femundsmarka				Gandvik	N	209	C8
				nasjonalpark	N	203	C8	Gardermoen	N	201	B7
				Festvåg	N	206	D4	Gaupne	N	202	E4
				Fetsund	N	201	C7	Geilo	N	200	A5
				Fevik	N	200	F5	Geiranger	N	202	C4
				Fillan	N	204	F2	Geithus	N	201	C6
				Finnøya	N	206	C4	Gibostad	N	208	E1
Ed	S	201	E8	Finnsnes	N	208	E1	Gideåkroken	S	205	D9
Edane	S	201	C9	Finnstad	N	203	C7	Gjermundshamn	N	200	B2
Edebäck	S	201	C9	Finse	N	200	A4	Gjerstad	N	201	E5
Edefors	S	207	F8	Fiskebäckskil	S	201	F7	Gjersvik	N	205	D6
Edsele	S	205	F8	Fiskebøl	N	206	B4	Gjesvær	N	209	A5
Egersund	N	200	E2	Fitjar	N	200	B2	Gjøra	N	203	B5
Eggedal	N	201	B6	Fjällbacka	S	201	E7	Gjøvik	N	201	A7
Eide	N	202	B4	Fjällnäs	S	203	B8	Gladstad	N	204	B5
Eidet	N	208	E1	Fjæra	N	200	B3	Glöte	S	203	D9
Eidfjord	N	200	A4	Fjærland	N	202	D3	Glomfjord	N	206	E3
Eidsdalen	N	202	C4	Fjordgård	N	208	D1	Gördalen	S	203	D8
Eidsvåg	N	202	B5	Flakaberg	S	207	F9	Görvik	S	205	F8
Eidsvoll	N	201	B7	Flakaträsk	S	205	B9	Gol	N	201	A5
Eidvågeid	N	208	B4	Flakstad	N	206	C3	Grästorp	S	201	F9
Eigerøya	N	200	E2	Flåm	N	202	F3	Gran	N	201	B7
Eikefjord	N	202	D2	Flatøydegard	N	203	F6	Granliden	S	205	D8
Eiken	N	200	E3	Flekkefjord	N	200	E3	Grannäs	S	205	B9
Eina	N	201	A7	Flesberg	N	201	C6	Gransherad	N	201	C5
Eivindvik	N	202	E2	Flesnes	N	206	B5	Granvin	N	200	A3
Ekenäs	S	201	E9	Flisa	N	201	A8	Gravberget	N	201	A8
Ekshärad	S	201	B9	Floby	S	201	F9	Grebbestad	S	201	E7
Elgå	N	203	C8	Flötningen	S	203	D8	Grimstad	N	200	F5
Ellös	S	201	F7	Florø	N	202	D2	Grövelsjön	S	203	C8
Elnesvågen	N	202	B4	Fluberg	N	201	A7	Grong	N	205	D5
Elsfjord	N	205	A6	Föllinge	S	205	F7	Grøtevær	N	206	A5
Elverum	N	201	A8	Foldereid	N	205	C5	Grotli	N	202	C4
Elvkroken	N	206	D5	Folkestad	N	202	C3	Grov	N	207	B5
Enge	N	203	A5	Follafors	N	204	E4	Grums	S	201	D9
Engerneset	N	203	E8	Folldal	N	203	C6	Grundträsk	S	207	F9
Enkodak	FIN	208	F5	Follebu	N	203	E6	Gryllefjord	N	207	A5
Enontekiö	FIN	208	F5	Førde	N	200	C2	Gubbträsk	S	205	C9
Erka	N	202	C5	Førde	N	202	D2	Gudvangen	N	202	E3
Espeland	N	200	A2	Formofoss	N	205	D5	Gullesfjordbotn	N	206	B5
Esrange	S	207	C8	Forneset	N	208	D2	Gulsvik	N	201	B6
Etne	N	200	C2	Forøya	N	206	F3	Gunnarn	S	205	C9
Evanger	N	200	A3	Forshaga	S	201	D9	Gunnarnes	N	208	A5
Evenskjer	N	207	B5	Forsmark	S	205	B8	Gunnfarnes	N	207	A5
Evertsberg	S	203	E9	Forsnes	N	204	F2	Gvarv	N	201	D5
Evje	N	200	E4	Forvika	N	205	B5				
Eydehavn	N	200	E5	Fosnavåg	N	202	C2				
				Fossbakken	N	207	B6				
				Fossli	N	200	A4				
				Fredrikstad	N	201	D7				
				Frihetsli	N	207	B7				
				Frosta	N	204	F4				
				Fulunäs	S	203	E9				
				Funäsdalen	S	203	C8	**H**ægeland	N	200	E4
				Furuflaten	N	208	D2	Häggenäs	S	205	F7
				Fusa	N	200	B2	Häggnäset	S	205	D7
Fåberg	N	202	D4	Fyresdal	N	200	D4	Hälla	S	205	E9
Fåberg	N	203	E6					Hällekis	S	201	E9
Färgelanda	S	201	E8					Håkafot	S	205	D7
Fagerås	S	201	D9					Hakkas	S	207	E9
Fagerhult	S	201	F8					Halden	N	201	D7
Fagernes	N	203	E5					Hallingdal	N	201	A5
Fagernes	N	208	D2					Hallviken	S	205	F8
Falköping	S	201	F9					Halsa	N	202	A5
Fana	N	200	B2					Halsvik	N	202	E2
Fannrem	N	203	A6					Hamar	N	201	A7

Name				Name				Name			
Kuttainen	S	208	F4	Likenäs	S	201	A9	Maura	N	201	B7
Kuttura	FIN	209	F7	Liknes	N	200	E3	Maurvangen	N	202	D5
Kvænangsbotn	N	208	D4	Lilla Edet	S	201	F8	Mavas	S	207	E5
Kvänum	S	201	F9	Lillehammer	N	203	E6	Mehamn	N	209	A7
Kvalsund	N	208	B5	Lillesand	N	200	F4	Melbu	N	206	B4
Kvam	N	203	D6	Lillestrøm	N	201	C7	Meldal	N	203	B6
Kvanndal	N	200	A3	Lima	S	201	A9	Melfjorden	N	206	F3
Kvelde	N	201	D6	Lindås	N	202	F2	Melhus	N	203	A7
Kvelia	N	205	D6	Lindesnes	N	200	F3	Mellerud	S	201	E8
Kvikkjokk	S	207	E6	Linge	N	202	C4	Menesjärvi	FIN	209	E7
Kvinlog	N	200	E3	Linsell	S	203	C9	Meråker	N	204	F5
Kviteseid	N	200	D5	Lisma	FIN	209	F6	Meselefors	S	205	D9
Kyrksæterøra	N	204	F2	Lit	S	205	F7	Messaure	S	207	F8
				Ljørndalen	N	203	E8	Messelt	N	203	E7
				Ljungdalen	S	203	B8	Midsund	N	202	B3
				Ljungskile	S	201	F8	Mieraslompolo	FIN	209	D7
				Løding	N	206	E4	Mierojokki	N	208	E4
				Lødingen	N	206	B5	Mikkelvik	N	208	C2
				Lödöse	S	201	F8	Misten	N	206	D4
				Lövberga	S	205	E8	Mittådalen	S	203	B8
				Lövnäs	S	203	E9	Mjönäs	S	201	C9
Lærdalsøyri	N	202	E4	Lövnäsvallen	S	203	D9	Mjøndalen	N	201	C6
Lævvajokgiedde	N	209	C6	Løfallstrand	N	200	B3	Mo	N	201	B8
Lahnajärvi	S	207	E9	Lofsdalen	S	203	C9	Mo i Rana	N	205	A7
Laimoluokta	S	207	C7	Lofthus	N	200	B3	Moelv	N	201	A7
Lainio	S	207	C9	Løken	N	201	C8	Moen	N	208	E1
Laisvall	S	205	A9	Løkken	N	203	A6	Mörkret	S	203	D8
Lakaträsk	S	207	F9	Lom	N	202	D5	Mörsil	S	205	F6
Lakfors	N	205	B6	Lomen	N	202	E5	Moi	N	200	E3
Lakselv	N	209	C5	Lonevåg	N	200	A2	Molde	N	202	B4
Lampeland	N	201	C6	Longyearbyen	N	198	B1	Mon	N	205	D6
Landön	S	205	F7	Loppa	N	208	C3	Mørsvik	N	206	D5
Långå	S	203	C9	Løten	N	201	A8	Mosby	N	200	F4
Langesund	N	201	D6	Lotta	RUS	209	E8	Mosjøen	N	205	B6
Langevåg	N	200	C2	Lund	N	204	D5	Moss	N	201	D7
Langevåg	N	202	B3	Lundamo	N	203	A7	Munkedal	S	201	F8
Langfjordbotn	N	208	C4	Lunde	N	201	D5	Murjek	S	207	F8
Långsjöby	S	205	C9	Luspebryggan	S	207	E7	Myckelgensjö	S	205	F9
Lannavaara	S	207	C9	Lyngdal	N	200	F3	Myrdal	N	200	A4
Lansjärv	S	207	F9	Lyngseidet	N	208	D2	Myre	N	206	B4
Lappuobbal	N	208	E5	Lysekil	S	201	F7	Myre	N	206	A5
Larkollen	N	201	D7	Lysnes	N	208	E1	Myrland	N	206	B5
Larseng	N	208	D1	Lysøysundet	N	204	E3	Myrlandshaugen	N	207	B6
Larvik	N	201	D6	Lysvik	N	201	C9	Myrmoen	N	203	B8
Laukvik	N	208	D1					Mysen	N	201	C7
Laukvika	N	206	D4								
Låveng	N	205	A6								
Lavik	N	202	E2								
Laxbäcken	S	205	D8								
Leikanger	N	202	C2								
Leikanger	N	202	E3								
Leipojärvi	S	207	E9								
Leira	N	202	A5	Magnor	N	201	C8				
Leira	N	203	F5	Malm	N	204	E4	Nabuvoll	N	203	C7
Leirbotn	N	208	C4	Malmberget	S	207	E8	Näätämö	FIN	209	C8
Leirmoen	N	206	F4	Måløy	N	202	C2	Nälden	S	205	F7
Leirpollskogen	N	209	B8	Malung	S	203	F9	Nærbø	N	200	F2
Leirvåg	N	202	E1	Malungsfors	S	201	A9	Namsos	N	204	D4
Leirvik	N	200	C2	Mandal	N	200	F3	Namsskogan	N	205	C6
Leirvik	N	208	C3	Mangen	N	201	C8	Narvik	N	207	B6
Leknes	N	202	C3	Manger	N	200	A2	Nattavaara	S	207	E9
Leknes	N	206	C3	Mardalen	N	202	C5	Naustdal	N	202	D2
Leksvik	N	204	F4	Marielund	S	205	B9	Nautijaur	S	207	E7
Lemmenjoki	FIN	209	E7	Markabygd	N	204	F4	Nautsi	RUS	209	D8
Lena	N	201	A7	Markkina	FIN	208	F4	Nedstrand	N	200	C2
Lervik	N	201	D7	Marvik	N	200	C3	Nelaug	N	200	E5
Levang	N	201	E5	Masfjorden	N	202	E2	Nellim	FIN	209	E8
Levanger	N	204	F4	Masi	N	208	D4	Nes	N	201	A6
Lidköping	S	201	F9	Masugnsbyn	S	207	D9	Nes	N	202	D3
Lidsjöberg	S	205	E7	Måsvik	N	208	C1	Nesbyen	N	201	A6
Lierbyen	N	201	C6	Maunu	S	208	F4	Nesflaten	N	200	C3

Nesheim	N	202	E2
Neslandsvatn	N	201	D5
Nesna	N	205	A6
Nesodden	N	201	C7
Nestavoll	N	203	C6
Nesttun	N	200	B2
Nesvik	N	200	D3
Nevlunghavn	N	201	E6
Nikel'	RUS	209	D9
Nikkaluokta	S	207	D7
Nilivaara	S	207	D9
Nissedal	N	200	D5
Nittedal	N	201	B7
Nodeland	N	200	F4
Nössemark	S	201	D8
Nord-Sel	N	203	D6
Nordagutu	N	201	D6
Norddal	N	202	D2
Nordfjordeid	N	202	C3
Nordfold	N	206	D4
Nordkjosbotn	N	208	E2
Nordmela	N	206	A4
Nordøyvågen	N	205	A5
Nordre Osen	N	203	E8
Noresund	N	201	B6
Norheimsund	N	200	B3
Norra Tresund	S	205	C8
Norråker	S	205	D8
Norrbäck	S	205	D9
Nossebro	S	201	F9
Notodden	N	201	C6
Nunnanen	FIN	209	F6
Nuorgam	FIN	209	C7
Nuvvus	FIN	209	C6
Ny Ålesund	N	198	A1
Nybergsund	N	203	E8
Nyneset	N	205	D5
Nyrud	N	209	D8
Nysäter	S	201	D9
Nyvoll	N	208	C4
Odda	N	200	B3
Öje	S	203	F9
Östmark	S	201	B9
Övre Soppero	S	207	C9
Okkelberg	N	204	F4
Øksfjord	N	208	C4
Okstad	N	203	A7
Oldeide	N	202	C2
Olden	N	202	D3
Olden	S	205	F6
Olderdalen	N	208	D3
Olderfjord	N	209	B5
Oldervik	N	208	D2
Ølen	N	200	C2
Oltedal	N	200	D2
Oppdal	N	203	B6
Ørje	N	201	D8
Orkanger	N	203	A6
Ørnes	N	206	E3
Orrliden	S	203	E9
Ørsta	N	202	C3
Ortnevik	N	202	E3
Os	N	203	C7
Ose	N	200	D4
Osen	N	204	D4
Oslo	N	201	C7
Osøyro	N	200	B2
Østby	N	203	E8
Oteren	N	208	E2
Otnes	N	203	D7
Otta	N	203	D6
Outakoski	FIN	209	D6
Øverdalen	N	202	C5
Øvergård	N	208	E2
Øvre Årdal	N	202	E4
Øvre Rendal	N	203	D7
Øye	N	202	E5
Øyslebø	N	200	F4
Pålkem	S	207	F9
Palojärvi	FIN	208	F5
Palojoensuu	FIN	208	F5
Palomaa	FIN	209	D7
Parakka	S	207	D9
Partakko	FIN	209	D8
Patoniva	FIN	209	C7
Peltovuoma	FIN	209	F5
Petsikko	FIN	209	D7
Pioltikasvaara	S	207	D8
Pokka	FIN	209	F6
Polmak	N	209	C7
Porjus	S	207	E8
Porsangermoen	N	209	C5
Porsgrunn	N	201	D6
Presteid	N	206	C4
Prestesætra	N	205	E5
Prestfoss	N	201	B6
Prirèènyj	RUS	209	D9
Pulju	FIN	209	F6
Pulsujärvi	S	207	B8
Puoltsa	S	207	D7
Pyhäjärvi	FIN	209	E6
Racksund	S	205	A9
Räsäker	S	205	F9
Raja-Jooseppi	FIN	209	E8
Rajakoski	RUS	209	D8
Rakkestad	N	201	D7
Ramsele	S	205	F8
Rånddalen	S	203	C9
Randijaur	S	207	E7
Randsverk	N	203	D5
Ranemsletta	N	204	D5
Raudeberg	N	202	C2
Raudlia	N	205	B7
Raufoss	N	201	A7
Rauland	N	200	C4
Reife	N	207	B6
Reine	N	206	C3
Reinsvik	N	202	A4
Reinsvoll	N	201	A7
Rena	N	203	E7
Rennebu	N	203	B6
Rensjön	S	207	C7
Repojoki	FIN	209	F6
Repvåg	N	209	B6
Revsnes	N	206	B5
Riksgränsen	S	207	B6
Rindal	N	203	B6
Rindbø	N	206	C5
Ringebu	N	203	D6
Risbäck	S	205	D8
Riska	N	200	D2
Risnes	N	200	E3
Risør	N	201	E5
Risøyhamn	N	206	A4
Rissa	N	204	F3
Ritsem	S	207	D6
Rjukan	N	200	C5
Roa	N	201	B7
Rødberg	N	201	B5
Rødsjøen	N	204	E3
Röjdåfors	S	201	B9
Rönäs	S	205	B7
Rönnöfors	S	205	F6
Rognan	N	206	E4
Rogne	N	203	E5
Røldal	N	200	C3
Røros	N	203	C7
Rørvik	N	204	C4
Rørvika	N	204	F3
Rosendal	N	200	B3
Rossön	S	205	E8
Røsvik	N	206	D4
Rottneros	S	201	C9
Roverud	N	201	B8
Røyken	N	201	C7
Røyrvik	N	205	C6
Rubbestadneset	N	200	B2
Rundfloen	N	203	E8
Ruokto	S	207	D7
Russelv	N	208	C2
Russnes	N	209	B5
Rusterfjelbma	N	209	B7
Rutledalen	N	202	E2
Rykene	N	200	E5
Rypefjord	N	208	B4
Rysjedalsvika	N	202	E2
Saariselkä	FIN	209	F7
Sæbø	N	202	C3
Säffle	S	201	D9
Sälen	S	203	E9
Särna	S	203	D9
Särvsjön	S	203	B9
Sævareid	N	200	B2
Sagvåg	N	200	C2
Saittarova	S	207	D9
Salhus	N	200	A2
Salmijärvi	RUS	209	C9
Salsbruket	N	204	D5
Sand	N	200	C3
Sand	N	201	B8
Sandane	N	202	D3
Sande	N	202	E2

Sandefjord	N	201	D6	Skjolden	N	202	D4	Stigen	S	201	E8
Sandnes	N	200	D2	Skjønhaug	N	201	C7	Stjørdal	N	204	F4
Sandnessjøen	N	205	A5	Skoghall	S	201	D9	Stødi	N	206	F4
Sandøysund	N	201	D6	Skogn	N	204	F4	Stöllet	S	201	B9
Sandsele	S	205	C9	Skollenborg	N	201	C6	Stöten	S	203	E9
Sandstad	N	204	F2	Skorovatn	N	205	D6	Stokkvågen	N	205	A6
Sandvika	N	204	F5	Skotterud	N	201	C8	Stokmarknes	N	206	B4
Sandvika	N	205	D6	Skreia	N	201	A7	Stonglandet	N	207	A5
Sandvikvåg	N	200	B2	Skrolsvika	N	207	A5	Stora Blåsjön	S	205	D7
Saraby	N	208	B4	Skudeneshavn	N	200	D2	Stordalen	N	202	C4
Sarpsborg	N	201	D7	Skulgam	N	208	D2	Stordalen	S	207	C7
Såtenäs	S	201	F9	Skutvika	N	206	C4	Stordalselv	N	208	D2
Sauda	N	200	C3	Skyttmon	S	205	F8	Store Molvik	N	209	A8
Sauland	N	201	C5	Slattum	N	201	C7	Storekorsnes	N	208	C4
Saxnäs	S	205	C7	Slidre	N	203	E5	Storelv	N	208	B4
Selbekken	N	204	F3	Slussfors	S	205	B8	Støren	N	203	B6
Selbu	N	203	A7	Smeberg	S	201	E8	Storforshei	N	205	A7
Selje	N	202	C2	Snåsa	N	205	E5	Storjola	S	205	C7
Seljebø	N	202	B5	Snillfjord	N	204	F3	Storjord	N	206	E4
Seljord	N	200	C5	Snøfjord	N	208	B5	Storjorda	N	206	F3
Selsjön	S	205	F9	Södra Tresund	S	205	C8	Storlien	S	203	A8
Setermoen	N	207	B6	Sörvattnet	S	203	C9	Storslett	N	208	D3
Sevettijarvi	FIN	209	D8	Sogndal	N	202	E3	Storstein	S	208	C3
Siebe	N	208	E4	Sokna	N	201	B6	Storsteinnes	N	208	E2
Siggerud	N	201	C7	Soknedal	N	203	B6	Storuman	S	205	C9
Siksjö	S	205	D9	Sola	N	200	D2	Stranda	S	202	C3
Siljan	N	201	D6	Solberg	S	205	E9	Strandebarm	N	200	B3
Sillerud	S	201	D8	Sollebrunn	S	201	F8	Straumen	N	204	E4
Silsand	N	208	E1	Sollihøgda	N	201	C7	Straumen	N	206	E4
Silvalen	N	205	A5	Sølsnes	N	202	B4	Straumen	N	206	E4
Sinnes	N	200	D3	Solsvik	N	200	A2	Straumen	N	208	E1
Sira	N	200	E3	Sommersete	N	209	B9	Straumsnes	N	206	B4
Sirevåg	N	200	E2	Søndeled	N	201	E5	Strimasund	S	205	A7
Sjoa	N	203	D6	Sør-Flatanger	N	204	D4	Strömstad	S	201	E7
Sjøasen	N	204	D4	Sør-Gutvika	N	204	C5	Strömsund	S	205	E8
Sjøholt	N	202	B3	Sør-Tverrfjord	N	208	C3	Stryn	N	202	C3
Sjøvegan	N	207	B6	Søre Moen	S	205	F5	Stuguflåten	N	202	C5
Sjuntorp	S	201	F8	Sørkjosen	N	208	D3	Sulitjelma	N	206	E5
Skärhamn	S	201	F7	Sørland	N	206	D2	Sunde	N	200	B2
Skaidi	N	209	B5	Sørli	N	205	E6	Sundnäs	S	205	A9
Skaitekojan	N	206	C5	Sørreisa	N	208	E1	Sunndal	N	200	B3
Skaitekojan	S	207	E8	Sørrollnes	N	207	B5	Sunndalsøra	N	202	B5
Skalltivaara	FIN	209	C7	Sorsele	S	205	B9	Sunne	S	201	C9
Skalmodal	S	205	B7	Sørstraumen	N	208	D3	Svanabyn	S	205	E9
Skalstugan	S	205	F5	Sortland	N	206	B4	Svanskog	S	201	D8
Skånevik	N	200	C2	Sørumsand	N	201	C7	Svanvik	N	209	C9
Skåningen	N	208	C2	Sørvær	N	208	B3	Svappavaara	S	207	D8
Skansnäs	S	205	B9	Sørvågen	N	206	C3	Svarstad	N	201	D6
Skara	S	201	F9	Sørvika	N	203	C8	Svatsum	N	203	E6
Skarberget	N	206	C5	Sotasæter	N	202	D4	Sveio	N	200	C2
Skardet	N	205	A7	Sparbu	N	204	E4	Svelgen	N	202	D2
Skardet	N	208	C3	Spjelkavik	N	202	B3	Svelvik	N	201	C7
Skare	N	200	B3	Stakkvik	N	208	D2	Svenes	N	200	E4
Skåre	N	201	D9	Staloluokta	S	207	E5	Svensby	N	208	D2
Skarness	N	201	B8	Stalon	S	205	C8	Svinndal	N	201	D7
Skarsvåg	N	209	A6	Stamnes	N	200	A3	Svolvær	N	206	C4
Skarvsjöby	S	205	C9	Stamsund	N	206	C3	Svorkmo	N	203	A6
Skatval	N	204	F4	Stange	N	201	A7	Svullrya	N	201	B8
Skaulo	N	207	D8	Stårheim	N	202	C2	Sykkylven	N	202	C3
Skeby	S	201	F9	Stathelle	N	201	D6	Sysslebäck	S	201	A9
Skedsmokorset	N	201	C7	Staume	N	202	D2				
Skee	S	201	E7	Stavanger	N	200	D2				
Skei	N	202	D3	Stavern	N	201	D6				
Skei	N	203	B5	Steine	N	206	B4				
Skei	N	204	C5	Steinkjer	N	204	E4				
Ski	N	201	C7	Steinshamn	N	202	B3				
Skibotn	N	208	E2	Stekenjokk	S	205	C7				
Skien	N	201	D6	Stensele	S	205	C9				
Skjelstad	N	204	E5	Stenträsk	S	207	F8				
Skjervøy	N	208	C3	Stenudden	S	207	F6				
Skjold	N	208	E2	Stenungsund	S	201	F8				

GENERAL INDEX

International dialing code for Norway from abroad
00 47

Emergency telephone numbers

Police:
Tel 112
Police from cell/mobile phone only:
Tel 911

Ambulance:
Tel 113

Fire:
Tel 110

Emergency at sea:
Tel 120

Tourist information

http://www.visitnorway.com
www.visitoslo.com/

Tourist offices in Norway
http://www.visitoslo.com/en/tourist-information-in-
   norway.58222.en.html

Rail information
http://www.eurail.com/eurail-railway-norway

Weather forecast
http://www.yr.no/place/Norway/

Car breakdown assistance
NAF (Norwegian Automobile Club):
For road assistance in Norway tel 08 505 (24 hour)
From abroad tel (+47) 926 08505
http://www.naf.no/en/

Viking Rescue Service:
Breakdown assistance tel 060 00 (24 hour)

Falck Rescue Service:
Breakdown assistance tel 022 22 (24 hour)

Information on driving in Norway
Norwegian Public Roads Administration
http://www.vegvesen.no/en/Traffic

Embassies and Consulates

American Embassy
Drammensveien 18
0244 Oslo
Tel (+47) 21 30 85 40
Fax (47) 22 56 27 51
Email: osloamcit@state.gov,
oslovisa@state.gov
http://www.usembassy.no/

Australian Consulate in Oslo
Wilh. Wilhelmsen ASA
Strandvn 20
Lysaker
(4 miles west of Oslo)
Tel (+47) 67 58 48 48
Fax (+47) 67 58 43 80
Email: Australian.embassy@mail.dk
http://www.dfat.gov.au/missions/countries/no.html

British Embassy
Thomas Heftyesgate 8
0264 Oslo
Tel (+47) 23 13 27 00
Fax (+47) 2313 2741
Email: britemb@online.no
http://ukinnorway.fco.gov.uk/en/

Embassy of Canada in Oslo
Wergelandsveien 7
0244 Oslo
Tel (+47) 22 99 53 00
Fax (+47) 22 99 53 01
Email: oslo@international.gc.ca
http://www.Norway.gc.ca

Embassy of Ireland in Norway
Haakon VIIs Gate 1
0244 Oslo
Tel (+47) 2201 7200
Fax (+47) 2201 7201
Email: osloembassy@dfa.ie
www.embassyofireland.no

South Africa Embassy in Oslo
Drammensveien 88 c
0271 Oslo
Tel (+47) 23 27 32 20
Fax (+47) 22 44 39 75
Email: sa-emb@online.no, amb@saemboslo.no,
oslo.reception@foreign.gov.za
http://www.saemboslo.no/

MONACO BOOKS is an imprint of Verlag Wolfgang Kunth

© Verlag Wolfgang Kunth GmbH & Co.KG, Munich, 2010
Concept: Wolfgang Kunth
Editing and design: Verlag Wolfgang Kunth GmbH & Co. KG
English translation: JMS Books LLP, design Caroline O 'Hara

For distribution please contact:

Monaco Books
c/o Wolfgang Kunth, Königinstraße 11
80539 München, Germany
Tel: (+49) 89 45 80 20 23
Fax: (+49) 89 45 80 20 21
info@kunth-verlag.de

www.monacobooks.com
www.kunth-verlag.de

ISBN 978-3-89944-574-9

Printed in Slovakia

All facts have been researched with the greatest possible care, to the best of
our knowledge and belief. However, the editors and publishers can accept no
responsibility for any inaccuracies or incompleteness of the details provided.
The publishers are pleased to receive any information or suggestions for
improvement.